English Language Teaching in a Neurodiverse World

From theory to neurodiversity-affirming practice

Dr Gemma Williams

Pavilion ELT

English Language Teaching in a Neurodiverse World

From theory to neurodiversity-affirming practice

Published by:
Pavilion Publishing and Media Ltd
Blue Sky Offices, 25 Cecil Pashley Way, Shoreham by Sea,
West Sussex, BN43 5FF

Tel: +44 (0)1273 434943
Email: info@pavpub.com
Web: www.pavpub.com

Published 2026

A catalogue record for this book is available from the British Library.

ISBN: 978-1-80388-518-6

Pavilion Publishing and Media is a leading publisher of books, training materials and digital content in mental health, social care and allied fields. Pavilion and its imprints offer must-have knowledge and innovative learning solutions underpinned by sound research and professional values.

Author: Dr Gemma Williams
Editor: Mike Benge
Cover design: Emma Dawe, Pavilion Publishing and Media Ltd
Page layout and typesetting: Emma Dawe, Pavilion Publishing and Media Ltd
Printing: Independent Publishers Group (IPG)

Contents

About the Author

Dr Gemma Williams is neurodivergent, with a deep interest in cognitive linguistics and neurodivergent communication; her doctoral research investigated communication between autistic and non-autistic speakers.

She is also an experienced EFL teacher with a Masters Degree in English Language Teaching. She has taught beginner level students through to advanced, business English learners to asylum seekers and migrant workers, from summer school groups to one-to-ones. Most recently, she has been involved in the production of digital ELT learning resources.

She is also the author of *Understanding Others in a Neurodiverse World* from Pavilion.

Acknowledgements

This work stands on the shoulders of all the neurodivergent activists and academics who have gone before.

With special thanks to – Lewis Shaw, for the late-night bouncing of ideas and the unwavering support. To Peter Mason, my ELT cheerleader and confidante. To Colette Thomson (of Sensations English) and Charlotte Rance (of OUP) for encouraging me to write this book. To Adam Scott (also of Sensations English) for the ELT pedagogy chats and cheer. And to Dr Andrew Blair and Dr Jules Winchester for inspiring me (all those years ago) during my MA in ELT to think critically and expansively about whose English we're teaching, when we're teaching English...

To Winnie and Goolie – thanks for the furry, cuddly companionship.

To the Pavilion ELT team – Ellie, Caitlin, and Mike – you've made it as easy as it could be, thank you!

For anyone who has ever felt 'different'...

Introduction

Welcome to *English Language Teaching in a Neurodiverse World*. If you're curious about neurodiversity and how it translates into the English language classroom, you've picked up the right book. Thank you for trusting me with that most precious of resources: your time.

One thing that almost all teachers I've ever spoken to have seem to have in common is an intrinsic motivation to support their students in their learning. Teachers *want* their learners to do well and spend hours reflecting on and refining their practice to ensure just that. As language teachers, caring deeply about the communicative development of our individual learners comes as much with the territory as a squeaky whiteboard marker and a trusty ice-breaker activity.

Precisely *because* every student's learning journey is unique, ELT professionals tend already to be experts at adapting materials, grading our language and planning out individualised learning targets. If there's one thing we know well, it's how to moderate our lessons and differentiate activities to meet the different needs of our learners. But even for the most experienced English language teacher, understanding how to anticipate and meet the needs of neurodivergent learners can feel a stretch too far.

For many, the language of neurodiversity has appeared in the vernacular seemingly out of nowhere and the breadth of unfamiliar terms and concepts can feel anything from daunting to overwhelming. Neurodiversity *isn't* new, but our awareness of it in education is still catching up – and this, I hope, is where this book comes in.

The good news, for you, is that many teachers are intuitively already making inclusive choices in the classroom – just without the terminology or frameworks to name them or ensure consistency. Having a solid understanding of neurodiversity and how it can play out in the classroom will really help to shore up and formalise the things many of you will already be doing.

Why this book and why right now

Humans have always processed the world around them in a range of ways. We are an endlessly varied species, adapting our cognition to work optimally in all kinds of different niches. However, it is only relatively recently that we've started to describe this propensity for different ways of thinking and experiencing the world as 'neurodiversity'.

The term 'neurodiversity' actually first started to come into use in the mid-1990s (more about that later, in Chapter 1) but it is really only in the past five years or so that common usage has boomed. From Siena Castellon's founding of the now globally recognised *Neurodiversity Celebration Week*[1] in 2018, through a perfect storm of online activism, a post-pandemic focus on mental health and growing awareness of disability inclusion in education and employment, 'neurodiversity' has suddenly become the buzzword on everyone's lips.

Despite the popularisation of the concept of neurodiversity, there remains something of a lag in terms of detailed, actionable understanding in most industries. Neurodiversity policies are still in development, or under revision, in businesses and organisations all around the world. For the ELT profession, clear, trustworthy and practical guidance is desperately needed. A general understanding of what neurodiversity means and entails is the first step in being able to meet our neurodivergent learners where they are. From here, ELT-specific, neurodivergent-led and evidence-backed insights for the classroom will enable teachers to work with – and not against – the unique strengths and challenges that at least a fifth of all students in every classroom will have (we will explore the numbers in more detail in Chapter 2).

1 Neurodiversity Celebration Week – the third week of March every year: www.neurodiversityweek.com

The need to make English language learning accessible to students with divergent needs is a moral one. However, as of July 2025, for teachers and institutions in the EU and the UK, accessibility is a legal requirement, too. The *European Accessibility Act (EAA)* came into effect on 28th June 2025, with the aim of legislating common accessibility standards for all products and services delivered across the European Union, ensuring they are accessible to disabled people: and neurodivergent needs are included under this directive.[2] This doesn't need to be an anxiety-fuelled tick-box exercise. It can be an opportunity to reach and support more learners, more fairly, and a chance for teachers to deepen our understanding of how different learners learn.

What to expect from this book

As teachers, we're really used to thinking in terms of lesson aims and objectives, but how often do you communicate those to your learners? For many teachers, sharing aims at the start of a lesson is second nature. For others, it's not something they often consider.

Knowing what to expect can really assist many neurodivergent learners to engage more fully with the tasks at hand as it removes some of the anxiety around trying to predict variables. It's an easy win – and who doesn't love an easy win?

Personally, I'm a massive fan of expectation-setting, and I like to try to practice what I preach, wherever I can, so here's what you can expect from this book…

The approach

Accessibility – and modelling accessibility – is a key concern in this book. As such, I'll aim, wherever possible, for a Plain English[3] writing style to make it as smooth a read as possible (although my neurodivergent brain does love a parenthesis!). Figures will have image descriptions written below them, and, to support those of you who prefer to skim-read or those who can't process lots of dense information at once, I've included TL:DR

---

2 *Directive (EU) 2019/882 of the European Parliament and of the Council of 17 April 2019 on the accessibility requirements for products and services.* Available at: https://eur-lex.europa.eu/legal-content/EN/TXT/?uri=CELEX%3A32019L0882 (accessed January 2026).

3 The Plain English Campaign, established in 1979, fights against the use of 'gobbledygook, jargon and misleading public information': www.plainenglish.co.uk

('Too long: didn't read') summaries at the end of every section, highlighting the key learning points. I've also provided the learning objectives at the start of each chapter to help with that expectation-setting.

All of the information contained within the following pages is grounded in up-to-date neurodiversity research. I'll share all relevant references and resources at the end of each chapter, so you can follow up on things that catch your interest. Crucially, though, as well as being research-informed, this book takes a *neurodiversity-affirming perspective* – one that respects and values neurodivergence as simply a different way of processing the world, rather than a collection of pathologised 'deficits'. Where it exists, I have prioritised research led by or involving openly neurodivergent researchers and neurodivergent-led theory. Anyone, of course, can do excellent research, and it's not to say that only neurodivergent people should research neurodiversity-related matters. However, there's something both morally right about giving a researched community a leading voice in research that concerns them (see the growing arguments for inclusive, *co-productive* research[4]) and scientifically enriching.[5]

Above all, I'll try to provide clear pathways from theory to practical adjustments and real-world classroom applications.

The structure

The aim of this book is to augment your understanding and build your confidence in supporting neurodivergent learners in the classroom.
To do this, in Section One, we'll begin at the beginning: exploring what 'neurodiversity' really means and unpicking its constituent parts. Chapter 1 introduces the concept of neurodiversity, reflecting on where the idea came from and who it includes. Chapter 2 looks in greater detail at some of the more common 'minority neurotypes' (for example, autism, ADHD, dyslexia etc.) that your learners may have, and demystifies terminology so that words and phrases like 'minority neurotype' and 'neurodiversity' can become comfortable parts of your vocabulary.

4 *Co-production* is a research methodology in which representative members of a researched community have a meaningful role in every stage of a research project: throughout design, delivery, evaluation and dissemination. See, e. g., Fletcher-Watson, S., Brook, K., Hallett, S., Murray, F. and Crompton, C.J. (2021) Inclusive practices for neurodevelopmental research. *Current Developmental Disorders Reports*, 8(2), pp.88-97.

5 For discussion, see Pellicano, E. (2020) Commentary: Broadening the research remit of participatory methods in autism science a commentary on Happé and Frith (2020). *Journal of Child Psychology and Psychiatry, and Allied Disciplines*, 61(3), 233–235. https:// doi.org/10.1111/jcpp.13212

Section Two brings our focus into the classroom. Chapter 3 considers meaningful inclusion and explores our legal responsibilities as teachers to deliver lessons that include everyone. Building on this, Chapter 4 introduces the concept of *Universal Design for Learning* (UDL) and looks at how this approach might be applied to ELT.

Section Three moves in closer still, and thinks about our neurodivergent learners as unique individuals with different needs. Chapter 5 presents three key theories about neurodivergent communicative differences and describes their relevance to ELT, while reflecting on the ways that many neurodivergent people *mask* (i.e. disguise) their neurodivergent traits. Chapter 6 thinks about whole learners (rather than collections of neurodivergent traits), by applying intersectional and decolonial lenses to neurodivergence.

Finally, in Section Four we move towards the practicalities of teaching for neurodiversity – and by that I mean not just teaching neurodivergent students but also helping them (as well as our neurotypical learners) ready themselves for navigating a neurodiverse world. Chapter 7 considers exactly this and focuses on the *pragmatic competence* needs of neurodivergent L2 communicators. Chapter 8 concludes the book by offering a walk-through of easy wins and small changes that teachers can adopt to improve accessibility for a wider range of learners – whatever their neurotype.

At the very end of the book, you'll find a resources list and a number of appendices featuring reflective tools for you to photocopy and use to extend your learning.

The author's positionality and background

Before we dive in, it might be helpful to hear just a little about who I am, and why I care so much about this subject.

First of all, I'm neurodivergent myself. Autism is the neurodivergence that most significantly shapes my day-to-day life, but I also experience many other neurodivergent traits outside of that diagnosis, including a nightmare with numbers, which I am certain is *dyscalculia* (worry not, we'll walk through these terms and neurotypes soon in the main body of the book).

I am also a cognitive linguist, with a deep interest in neurodivergent communication. My doctoral research investigated communication between autistic and non-autistic speakers from the perspective of *relevance theory* – something I've written about in detail in my book *Understanding Others in a Neurodiverse World*[6] – and I've gone on to research all manner of neurodiversity-related topics[7] since then, which have refined my understanding of the lived experience of people with minority neurotypes.

Finally, I am also an experienced EFL (English as a foreign language) teacher with a deep interest in pedagogy and a Masters Degree in English Language Teaching. I've taught from beginner level students through to advanced, business English learners to asylum seekers and migrant workers, from summer school groups to one-to-ones. Most recently, I've been involved in the production of digital ELT learning resources. Whoever the learners, it's always been a great privilege to be part of their journey and I'm really grateful to join you on yours, too.

Let's go!

My hope is that this book provides you not just with information, but also encouragement and confidence. Supporting neurodivergent students doesn't mean reinventing your practice: just thinking about it in (potentially) new ways. Many of you will already be doing lots of things that support your neurodivergent learners. All that's needed is a little additional underlying theory and some structure…

So, whether you're reading cover to cover or dipping in and out, I hope you find ideas here that affirm what you're already doing and plant the seeds of new ways to support every learner in your classroom.

Are you ready? Let's begin.

---

6 Wiliams, G.L. (2024) *Understanding Others in a Neurodiverse World: A radical perspective on communication and shared meaning.* Pavilion Publishing.

7 Most of these research papers have been published *Open Access* – i.e. freely available to read and not behind a journal's paywall. You can find them here: https://linktr.ee/drgemmawilliams

Section One

Neurodiversity

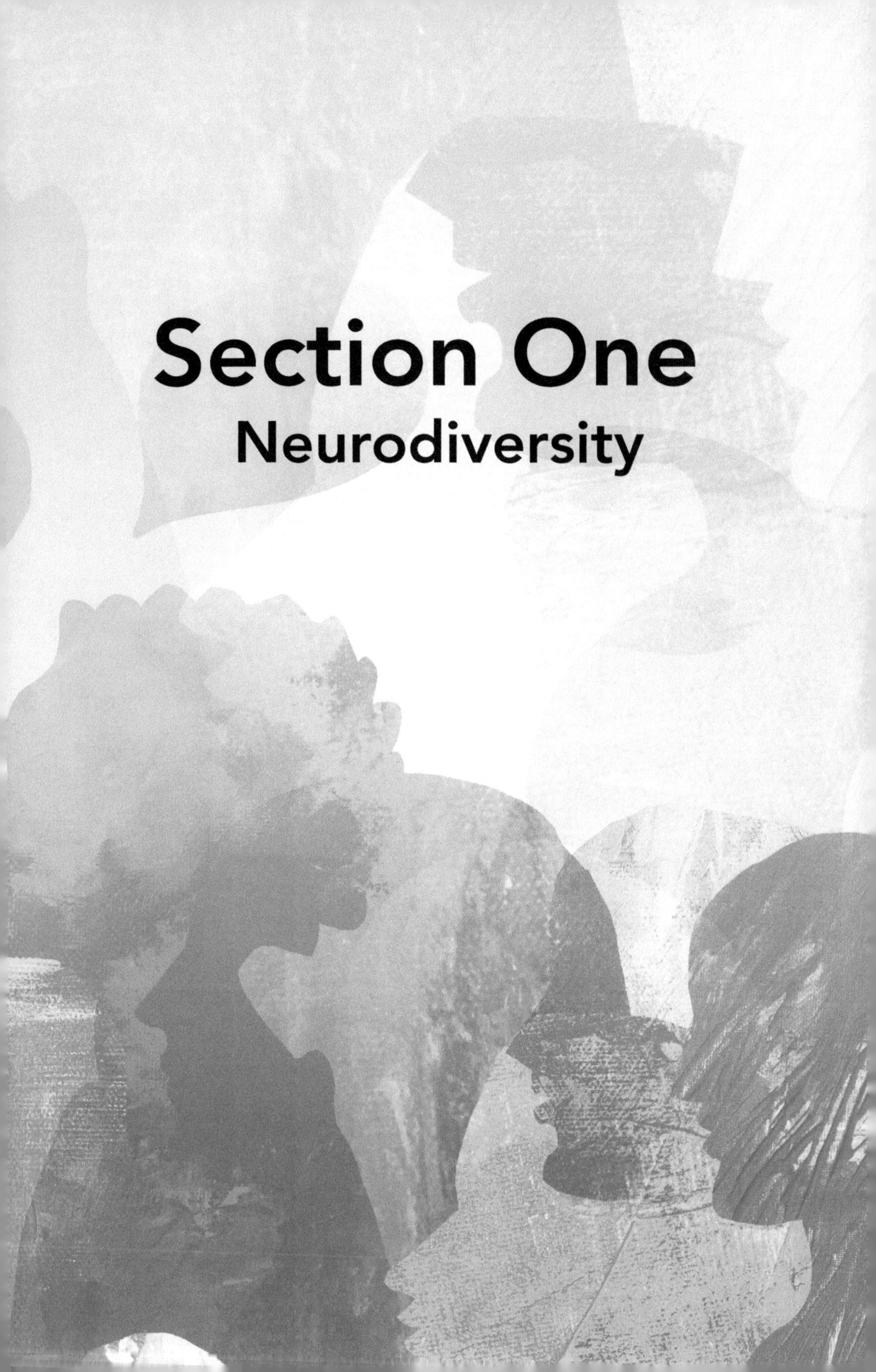

Chapter 1: What is 'neurodiversity'?

By the end of this chapter you'll be able to:

- differentiate key neurodiversity terminology
- define neurodiversity
- explain who and what is included when we talk about neurodivergence
- contextualise the neurodiversity concept within the history of the neurodiversity movement
- recognise the social and medical models of disability.

To talk about neurodiversity with the kind of precision and nuance we'll need throughout the rest of the book, it's important to first establish a shared understanding of some key terms. As language teachers, we know how much words matter, so this seems a sensible place to begin.

Most of the following terms are fairly intuitive for those with a flair for derivations, but often get confused in general usage. The most common term – 'neurodiverse' – is, for example, often mistakenly used in the place of 'neurodivergent'. Some – but not all – neurodivergent people feel strongly about the correct words being used to describe them. This most likely has its roots in a long history of pathologising and sometimes dehumanising language being used to describe neurodivergent individuals[8]. In one recent UK-based survey study exploring neurodivergent adults' views of neurodiversity-related terminology, for example, many respondents expressed discomfort with the misuse of the terms above.[9] For some, neurodiversity-related words being used incorrectly was interpreted as a sign of insincere lip-service to inclusion on the part of the speaker, as opposed to genuine care and consideration of neurodivergence.

However, it can take some time to acclimatise to the granularity of the different meanings. If it takes a while to become familiar with them, or if you slip up, don't worry; it's really not the end of the world. As long as your intentions are good, learners and colleagues will appreciate your efforts.

Key terminology

Neurodiversity (noun)
The natural variation in human cognition – in particular the variety of ways of thinking, learning, processing, and experiencing the world. For example: 'Recognising **neurodiversity** helps us teach more inclusively'.

Neurotype (noun)
A person's inherent way of thinking, processing, and experiencing the world. Everyone has a neurotype – these are often described as 'typical' or atypical. For example: 'A learner's **neurotype** will influence how they learn and communicate'.

Neurodiverse (adjective)
Describes a group of people who have a range of different neurotypes. An individual is not neurodiverse. For example: 'We are proud to have a **neurodiverse** teaching faculty in our school'.

Neurodivergence (noun)
The different patterns of cognition people can have – i.e. different ways of thinking, learning, behaving and processing sensory information –

8 Pearson, A., Grant, A., Leigh, J., Macdonald, S., Williams, K., Williams, G., Spaeth, E., Rose, K., Memmott, A. & Botha, M. (2025) 'It's like calling short people vertically challenged': Language and terminology preferences among neurodivergent adults. doi:10.31219/osf.io/jf62e_v1.

9 Grant *et al.* (2025) 'A lovely safe umbrella to describe yourself with' or 'meaningless': an online survey of UK-based Neurodivergent adults' views of neurodiversity-related terminology. *Neurodiversity*, 3, p.27546330251390590.

that differ from the assumed 'typical' or 'normative' way. For example: '**Neurodivergence** can influence how learners process spoken instructions'.

Neurodivergent (or, ND) (adjective)
The characteristic of processing information differently from the majority. An individual can be neurodivergent (or neurotypical – see below). For example: '**Neurodivergent** students may require addition supports or adjustments'.

Neurotypical (or NT) (adjective)
The characteristic of processing information in ways that align with societal expectations of what is 'typical' or 'standard'. For example: 'Most coursebooks assume a **neurotypical** pace and attention span'.

Neurotypical (noun)
A neurotypical person. For example, 'The activities have been designed by, and implicitly for, **neurotypicals**'.

Minority neurotype/neurominority (noun phrase/noun)
A neurodivergent neurotype – with an emphasis on the marginalisation that those with atypical neurotypes can experience. Examples: 'Students with **minority neurotypes** often face unmet needs in the classroom' and '**Neurominorities** are calling for inclusive teaching practices'.

Neurodiversity: In more depth

Now that we have the language clear, it's important, I think, before we can properly explore the practicalities of neurodiversity-inclusive English language teaching, to first spend some time unpacking the concept of neurodiversity.

It may come a surprise to some readers, but humans have been neurodiverse for as long as there have been humans. The *fact* of neurodiversity is not new. What's changed is perhaps its *relevance*, which has increased in recent times in response to a culture of intensifying capitalism with increasingly homogenising norms.[10] As social norms and expectations became more restricting (and tied to productivity), new

10 See Robert Chapman's *Empire of Normality* for an excellent analysis of 'normality' and neurodiversity in the context of the capitalism's 'production machine'.

descriptors were required to classify those who didn't make the grade. Certainly, the naming of neurodiversity and the understanding and reifying of it as such is a very recent phenomenon.

Whole books have been written exploring the concept of neurodiversity from different angles and lenses. Medical doctors, philosophers, activists, psychiatrists, self-advocates and researchers from all manner of disciplines have had – sometimes contradictory – things to say about it. But while some aspects may appear to be in flux, the central idea remains consistent. If I had to give you a single line to summarise this central idea, I would say this: *neurodiversity describes the different ways that people process and experience the world around them.*

Who counts as neurodivergent?

As yet, there is no universally agreed-upon definition for who counts as 'neurodivergent'. In part, this is because neurodiversity refers to a broad and evolving framework for understanding human cognitive variation: and one that is informed by a range of different, sometimes conflicting, perspectives that are also culturally shaped. At the time of writing, the generally accepted figures are that around 15-20% of people have some kind of neurodivergence, though I would urge caution in taking this as fact. Figures such as these are based on formal medical diagnoses of neurodivergent conditions (such as autism, ADHD, dyslexia, etc). Many people face significant societal and cultural barriers to accessing formal diagnoses – this has historically been especially the case for Black, Brown and Asian people, women and girls, older adults and those living in countries where neurodivergence is conceptualised differently. Others may choose not to seek them out due to stigma, or lack of understanding. As such, I personally suspect the neurodivergent population is far larger than we currently estimate.

Combining 'neurological' (see below) and 'diversity', 'neurodiversity' is a portmanteau tipping its hat at the word 'biodiversity'. Baked into the heart of the concept of neurodiversity, then, is the starting position that, much like with *biodiversity* (where we need lots of different kinds of organisms for an ecosystem to thrive), human societies benefit from neurological variety. All kinds of minds are seen as unique and uniquely valuable. The neurodiversity concept is therefore inherently validating and supportive of atypical ways of thinking, learning and communicating.

However, it is also important to note that, in the UK (and many other countries), diagnoseable neurodivergent conditions are classed as a disability, in recognition of the significant challenges that many neurodivergent people experience. That said, not all neurodivergent people will choose to self-identify as disabled. As will often be my advice, if you're unsure how someone prefers to describe themselves, ask them, or follow their lead.

Aa Terminology note: Neurological

'Neurological', in its truest sense, is a medical term describing (disease or damage to) the physical structures and biological functioning of the nervous system and brain. In lay terms, it's often used to refer to the brain and cognition. 'Neurodivergence', in fact, really has more to do with cognition and processes related to thinking, attention, language, memory, learning and perception – and rarely involves consistent neurological markers.

While 'cognitive differences' is probably the most correct description of neurodivergence, you'll often still see this used interchangeably with 'neurological differences', by both self-advocates and professionals.

A brief history of the neurodiversity paradigm

Use of the term 'neurodiversity' has boomed only in very recent years. According to Google Ngram Viewer[11], the word 'neurodiversity' first started appearing in published books around 1998: with usage growing roughly ten-fold by 2005 and then further four-fold from then until 2020. It's really since just around 2020 that its usage has begun to soar.

11 A tool that tracks the frequency of words or phrases across a vast corpus of digitised books. This a really fun tool and a great way to familiarise yourself with analysing corpora. Try it here: https://books.google.com/ngrams/

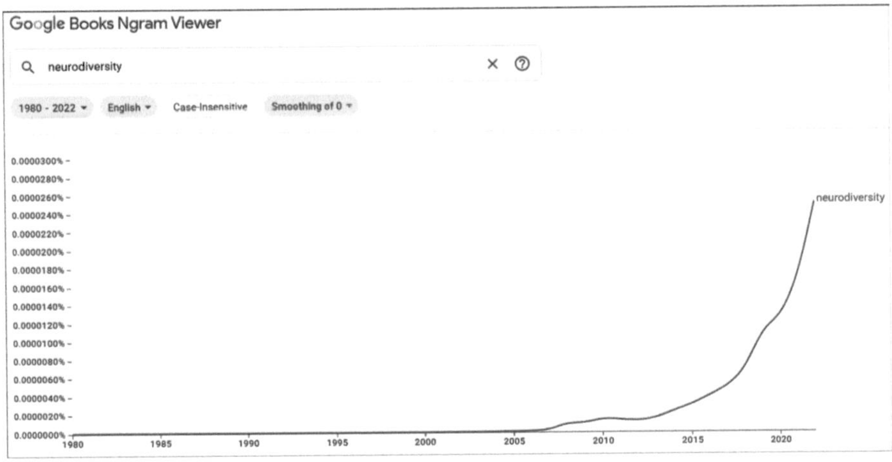

Figure 1.1: A graph shows the usage of the word 'neurodiversity' in published books, from 1980-2022. Data source – Google Ngrams

The term may be relatively new in public discourse, but the ideas behind it have been developing for decades, especially in disability justice spaces and in the steadily growing body of neurodivergent scholarship and advocacy.

Origins

Traditionally, the coining of the term 'neurodiversity' has been attributed to Australian autistic researcher Judy Singer, who used the term in her Honours thesis, an extract of which was published in 1999.[12] However, more recent archivist research has located the term as something that emerged more fluidly in the mid-1990s across the 'Independent Living' email list, where autistic and neurodivergent members often discussed in long email threads the idea of 'neurological diversity'.[13]

The neurodiversity paradigm itself also has its footing in these online disability-activist forums that had begun to emerge in the 1990s, as public access to the internet facilitated a surge of online community-building. In the first instance, it was autistic individuals on dedicated email lists and chat boards who began to find one another and organise a nascent autism rights movement. This, it's important to remember,

12 Singer, J. (1999) Why can't you be normal for once in your life? From a 'problem with no name' to a new category of disability. In: M. Corker & S. French (Eds.), *Disability Discourse* (pp. 59–67). Open University Press.

13 Botha, M., Chapman, R., Giwa Onaiwu, M., Kapp, S.K., Stannard Ashley, A. & Walker, N. (2024) The neurodiversity concept was developed collectively: An overdue correction on the origins of neurodiversity theory. *Autism*, 28(6), pp.1591-1594.

was happening against a backdrop of stigma and pity directed at autistic people at the time, with autism (and, by extension, any other disabling neuro-cognitive conditions) seen as a 'tragedy' that needed to be mourned.[14] Responding to this, American autistic rights activist Jim Sinclair gave what is now considered a watermark speech at the 1993 International Conference on Autism in Toronto, Canada. Addressing parents of autistic children, Sinclair urged, '...radical changes in your perceptions of what autism means. I invite you to look at our autism, and look at your grief, from our perspective.'[15] As the autism rights movement picked up momentum, a broader, sister *neurodiversity movement* developed that took under its wing the wider range of neurodivergences,[16] and the *neurodiversity paradigm* was born.

Terminology note:
Neurodiversity *paradigm* vs. *movement*

While the neurodiversity paradigm is a theoretical framework, the neurodiversity movement refers to the social and political campaign (in the loosest sense) for justice, full societal inclusion, and civil rights for neurodivergent people.

As with any social justice movement, the neurodiversity movement comprises a broad range of people and organisations with varying perspectives and goals.

The social and medical models of disability (and neurodiversity)

The early 1990s was a fertile time for the formation of neurodiversity activism. Not only were disabled and neurodivergent people now finding and building communities online, but the broader disability rights movement had begun to organise itself just a few years before, in the 1980s.

14 Kapp, S.K. (ed.) (2020) *Autistic community and the neurodiversity movement: Stories from the frontline* (p. 330). Springer Nature/Palgrave MacMillan.

15 You can read Jim Sinclair's full 'Don't Mourn For Us' speech at www.autreat.com/dont_mourn.html

16 Walker, N. (2021) *Neuroqueer Heresies: Notes on the neurodiversity paradigm, autistic empowerment, and postnormal possibilities.* Fort Worth, TX: Autonomous Press.

At the time, the predominant attitude towards disability was one that was highly influenced by what's often referred to as the 'medical model of disability'. The medical model – which still monopolises diagnostic and healthcare frameworks today – understands physical, mental and cognitive difference as conditions, disorders and dysfunction. The property of *disablement*, through this lens, is seen as belonging to an individual disabled person whose differences are, essentially, impairments that medical intervention can sometimes aid.

Out of the burgeoning disability rights movement of the 1980s came a counter-narrative, coined the 'social model of disability' by disabled activist and sociologist Mike Oliver in 1983.[17] Challenging the perspective of the prevailing medical model, disabled people began to make the argument that their disablement, in fact, came from the ways in which society treated them and from the systemic lack of equitable access.

Disabling barriers can and do take many forms. They may be physical (for example, the absence of wheelchair-accessible toilets), social (for example, dehumanising assumptions about a person's capacity or ability), cultural (for example, a lack of signers or closed captions for Deaf attendees at events), or financial (for example, services priced beyond the reach of those relying on disability benefits). What matters is that many of these can be circumvented by the provision of appropriate accommodations, adjustments or services.

Such accommodations or adjustments are exactly the kind of (often) small changes you can make in the language classroom to help to remove or reduce disabling barriers to your neurodivergent learners. Dyslexic learners who experience anxiety and difficulty reading aloud in front of a group aren't limited by their dyslexia, but by inaccessible resources and activities. Autistic learners who find loud, fast-paced group activities overwhelming, aren't unable to participate due to their autism, but due to the sensory environment. Learners with ADHD who miss classes or lose focus aren't inherently disinterested, they're struggling with a lack of supportive structure.

It's important to emphasise here that neither the social model of disability nor the neurodiversity paradigm overlook the difficulties that many disabled and neurodivergent people experience. Both

17 Oliver, M. (1983) Social Work with Disabled People. *Practical Social Work Series*, BASW.

perspectives recognise that being neurodivergent can be disabling. However, they see these challenges as the result of systems and environments that weren't created to accommodate different needs, rather than as individual impairments.

The understanding that disability arises from the interaction between a person and their environment lies at the heart of the social model of disability and, similarly, runs right through the concept of neurodiversity. When we move our attention away from trying to change the person and instead focus on changing the environment, new opportunities open up. We can ask different questions, such as how can I make this space easier for everyone to use? What ideas might I be holding about how people pay attention, take part or communicate? Who might be being left out by the usual way things are done?

Types of neurodivergence

There is just one final thing to clarify before we move on to looking at different minority neurotypes in more detail in the next chapter. Most of the time when people talk about 'neurodivergence', they're talking about things like autism, ADHD, dyslexia, etc. However, neurodivergence – differences in ways of processing, thinking, learning, perceiving and communicating – is actually rather broader than that and tends to fall into two main clusters: *developmental* and *acquired*.

- **Developmental neurodivergence** is the kind we're perhaps most familiar with. This category includes differences in cognition that are typically present from birth or very early in life and tend to affect learning, communication, attention, movement and/or sensory processing. These minority neurotypes are often referred to in clinical settings as 'neurodevelopmental disorders', although many neurodivergent advocates and scholars prefer terms such as 'neurodevelopmental differences', or 'profiles'. Some examples you may have heard of (which we'll look at in close detail in Chapter 2) include autism, ADHD, dyslexia and Tourette's.
- **Acquired neurodivergence** refers to changes in cognitive functioning and behaviour that arise later in life, often as a result of injury (such a traumatic brain injury or a stroke), illness (such as dementia or Alzheimer's), or environmental factors (including trauma).

> In some cases, acquired neurodivergence is temporary and resolves with medical or pharmaceutical intervention, or as an injury heals. Also worth noting is that – albeit less commonly – some definitions of acquired neurodivergence also include people with experiences such as hearing voices (for example, in the case of schizophrenia or post-traumatic stress disorder (PTSD)), or those living with complex mental health diagnoses.

This chapter's purpose has been to help us better understand neurodiversity — what it is, its history, the different groups it covers, and the key terminology used to talk about it. In the following chapter, we'll look more closely at distinct minority neurotypes and think about key strengths and challenges.

Finally, here is your first TL:DR summary, as promised. As I described in the introduction, modelling accessibility as best I can has been an important part of the construction of this book. Short summaries like these at the end of chapters or sections can be supportive in a number of ways. Some neurodivergent people struggle to process lots of new information at once. Others may have working memory problems. Others still might find large blocks of text hard to parse. Bulleted summaries allow readers to access and refer back to the key points quickly. As with most accessibility accommodations, they're often helpful for readers who might consider themselves neurotypical, too.

TL:DR (too long: didn't read) summary

- 'Neurodiversity' describes the different ways that people process and experience the world around them.
- It refers to the full range of human cognitive variation in perception, learning, and communication – including both neurotypical and neurodivergent people.
- 'Neurodivergence' describes the ways some people's cognition diverges from dominant expectations. There are many kinds of neurodivergence and they can be either developmental or acquired.

- The neurodiversity paradigm frames cognitive differences as natural and valuable, although it also recognises that neurodivergent experiences can be disabling. This is not necessarily because of the difference itself, but often because of the mismatch between individuals and the environments, systems or expectations they're navigating.
- The social model of disability shaped the neurodiversity paradigm and movement. It is a way of thinking about disability and neurodiversity that shifts the focus from individual 'deficits' to societal barriers.

Reflective questions

1. What neurodiversity terms have you encountered in the past that have felt unclear? How could you clarify these for your learners?
2. How have your own ideas about 'normal' behaviour, attention or communication been shaped by your training or teaching context?
3. Can you think of a time when a student's needs or behaviours were pathologised in a way that now seems avoidable or unhelpful?
4. What small changes could you make in your classroom or materials to build a culture more inclusive of difference?

Chapter 2: The spectrum of neurodivergence

By the end of this chapter you'll be able to:

- distinguish and describe the most common kinds of developmental neurodivergence
- recognise the diversity and individuality within each neurotype
- apply your understanding of these neurodivergent profiles to the context of a language teaching classroom.

Now that we've spent some time getting to grips with the foundations of the neurodiversity paradigm – what neurodiversity means, who it includes, how it developed – we can begin to think about distinct neurodivergent profiles.

As we've seen in the previous chapter, neurodivergence is a broad umbrella, encompassing all manner of atypicalities in the domains of cognition, sensory processing, communication, learning and attention. Each of the minority neurotypes dealt with in this chapter will have a unique pattern of difference across these domains – and these differences are the basis of formal (or self) diagnoses. However, every neurodivergent person is unique and their neurodivergence will manifest in slightly different ways. Moreover, neurodivergence is just one small part of a person's identity and will be shaped by many of the other factors that make the individual who they are (something we'll look at more closely in Chapter 6). Finally, it is quite common an individual to be *multiply neurodivergent*; that is, to have a number of coexisting neurodivergences.

In focus: Formal diagnosis vs self-diagnosis

With the growing global awareness of neurodiversity, we have also seen a growing number of formal diagnoses being made of neurodivergent conditions, especially of autism and ADHD. This reflects our greater understanding and the resultant amendments to diagnostic criteria rather than an increase in the number of neurodivergent people.

However, many neurodivergent people still do not have access to formal diagnoses. This may be due to the many diagnostic biases related to gender, ethnicity, age or intellectual abilities. For others it may be that, in their country, healthcare costs are too prohibitive, or that diagnoses are still stigmatised. Even in countries where healthcare is free, like in the UK, the wait times for diagnostic assessment can span years.

Because of this, there are many people who do not have a formal diagnosis but instead identify as being neurodivergent. This is often referred to as *self-diagnosis* and is widely accepted within the neurodiversity movement as an important part of self-advocacy.

In the following sections, we'll work alphabetically through some of the most common kinds of developmental neurodivergence: the kinds that you are likely to encounter in your language classrooms. As we do, we'll be guided by a neurodiversity-affirming approach: one that seeks to understand learners in terms of difference, not deficit, and that recognises both strengths and challenges.

These are broad snapshots rather than exhaustive descriptions, intended not for armchair diagnoses, but to help you better understand and support the diverse range of neurocognitive experiences your learners may bring to the classroom. One final caveat to add is that, while I'm sharing with you the commonly accepted prevalence rates for each neurodivergence as a guide, do take these with a pinch of salt, for the reasons explained in Chapter 1.

ADHD (Attention Deficit Hyperactivity Disorder)

What it is

ADHD is a developmental neurodivergence characterised by differences in attention regulation, impulse control and activity levels. It's often misunderstood as simply 'hyperactivity' or 'inattentiveness', but ADHD significantly shapes how a person experiences and interacts with their environment. It reflects variations in something called *executive functioning* – the brain's system for managing focus, self-control, task management and organisation – rather than a lack of effort or motivation.

ADHD presents in three main types: *predominantly inattentive*, *predominantly hyperactive-impulsive*, or *combined type*. Some people mainly struggle with attention and focus, others with high energy and impulsivity, and many experience a combination of both.

In the public eye: American Olympic gymnast Simone Biles.

Terminology note: *Disorder, syndrome, condition*

Because formal diagnoses of neurodivergence (at least for now) come from a medical paradigm, the names used to describe them often include medicalised words like 'disorder', 'syndrome' or 'condition'.

The pathologising nature of these and similar terms doesn't align well with the principles of neurodiversity: where the preferred words talk about *difference* instead of *deficits*. However, because this is the language of formal diagnoses, it's sometimes hard to avoid.

I've included them here where they are part of formal diagnostic labels, for your information. However, it is worth being mindful when talking to neurodivergent individuals of how language choices may affect how they feel about themselves.

Prevalence

Approximately 5% of the population are identified as having ADHD, although until very recently it has mostly been children receiving formal ADHD diagnoses. We now know that developmental neurodivergence is lifelong and continues into adulthood. While some hyperactive behaviours may decrease over time, differences in attention and impulsivity typically remain. However, ADHD traits are sometimes more invisible in adulthood because they are *masked*. Girls, too, are often underdiagnosed because their experiences may look less typical or be overlooked.

Aa Terminology note: *Masking*

Masking or *camouflaging* describes the 'conscious or unconscious suppression or projection of aspects of self and identity, and the use of non-native cognitive or social strategies' that neurodivergent people use to preserve their safety.[18]

In other words, many neurodivergent people find they moderate their neurodivergent traits to try to better blend into a world that has historically judged and treated them poorly.

Strengths

People with ADHD often have exceptional creativity and innovative thinking. Their ability to form unconventional connections can lead to novel problem-solving approaches. Many experience *hyperfocus* (more on this in Chapter 5) allowing them to intensely concentrate on tasks they find meaningful or interesting, resulting in high productivity or expertise. Their natural enthusiasm and energy often inspire and motivate those around them.

Challenges

Sustained attention on lengthy or multi-step activities can be difficult, making it harder to complete written tasks or follow complex instructions over extended periods of time. Impulsivity might cause spontaneous

18 Pearson, A. & Rose, K. (2023) *Autistic Masking: Understanding identity management and the role of stigma*. Pavilion Publishing.

interruptions or blurting out answers, sometimes impacting social dynamics in the classroom. Organisation and time management may also present challenges, leading to missed deadlines or forgotten tasks.

Example student

Khalil eagerly participates in class discussions and shows strong verbal skills, but he finds it difficult to sustain attention long enough to complete writing assignments. He's the class joker and is well-liked but sometimes disruptive to the flow of the lesson. His verbal fluency contrasts with struggles during independent work, and he often 'checks out' mid-activity, turning to look at his phone.

Autism (ASD- Autism Spectrum Disorder)

What it is

Autism is a developmental neurodivergence that affects how people communicate, process sensory information and organise their thinking and behaviour. Autism presents differently from person to person meaning that no two autistic students will have exactly the same pattern of autistic traits. A common expression, attributed to autistic academic Prof Stephen Shore, is that 'if you've met one autistic person... you've met one autistic person...'

However, on the whole, autistic people tend to experience some form of difference in social communication, sensory processing (being more sensitive or less sensitive to sights, sounds, touch and other sensory input), motor skills and executive functioning.

The idea of the 'spectrum' is also often misinterpreted in the public understanding of autism. Usually, the *autism spectrum* is thought of as quite linear – from what has sometimes been described 'low-functioning' to high-functioning' – with individual autistic people sitting somewhere along that line, like this:

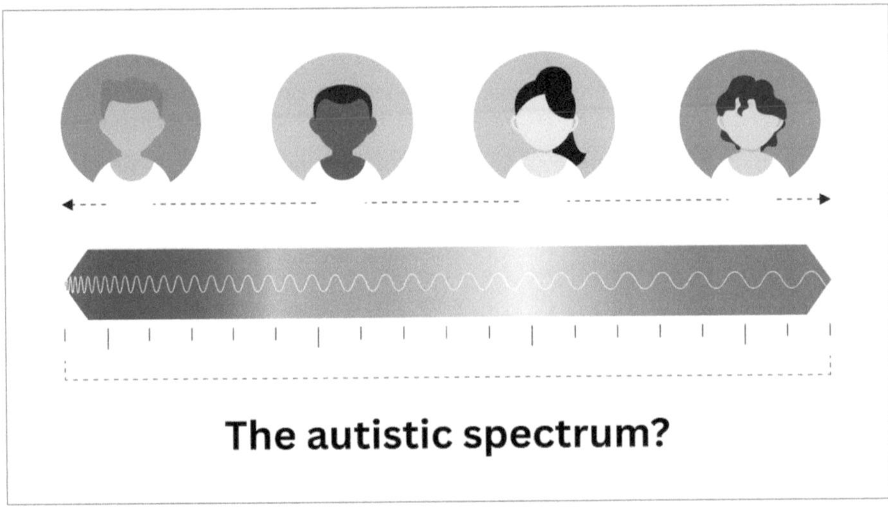

Figure 2.1: A visual depiction of a linear autism spectrum. Four people are placed along a rainbow-coloured line, to show their position along it.

In fact, it's more that each autistic person has their own unique spectrum of autistic traits, like this:

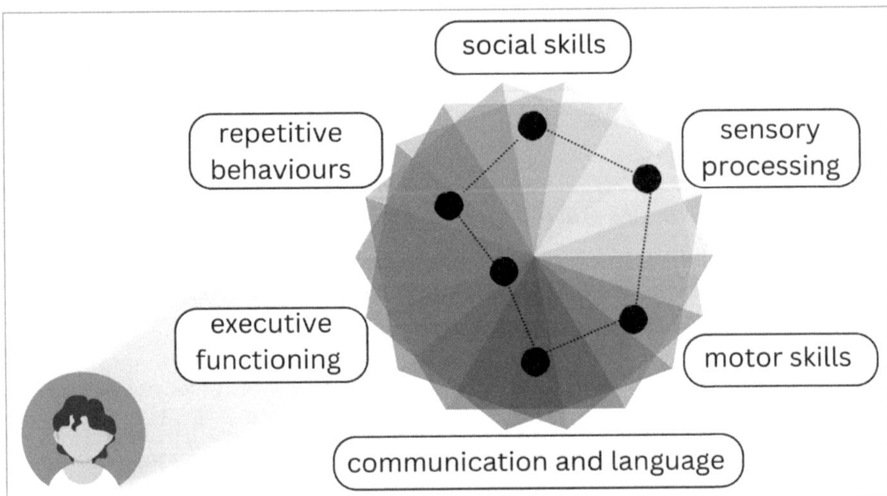

Figure 2.2: A visual depiction of one person's autistic traits. Six different labelled domains are represented as being stronger or weaker, with dots placed closer or further into the middle of a rainbow-coloured circle.

This means that some autistic people will need a lot of support to live independently, whereas others will need less regular support, but will still experience difficulties in different areas at certain times. This is why the terms 'low-functioning' and 'high-functioning' are no longer preferred: because a person's ability to function and perform certain tasks can vary from moment to moment, dependent on the environment.

In the public eye: UK naturalist and environmental campaigner Chris Packham.

Prevalence

Current estimates put the prevalence of autism at around 1% to 2% of the population, although this is likely an underestimate due to historical underdiagnosis and the diagnostic biases highlighted in the previous chapter.

Strengths

Autistic learners often have exceptional attention to detail and strong pattern recognition, which can be a huge asset in language learning, especially in areas like grammar and vocabulary. Many have an excellent memory for facts and specific details, sometimes called *encyclopaedic memory*, particularly when their interest is engaged. Their focused interests and unique perspectives can lead to creativity and deep passion, driving intense engagement with topics they care about. Autistic people sometimes have a tendency towards systematic and logical thinking, which can support effective problem-solving.

Challenges

Sensory sensitivities can make public spaces – like busy or noisy classrooms – overwhelming, which may affect concentration and comfort. Vague or implicit instructions can cause confusion, so clear, direct communication is important. Social group work might be difficult due to challenges in interpreting social cues or understanding unspoken rules. Motor coordination differences may also affect handwriting or the use of certain technologies.

Example student

Myriam excels in grammar exercises requiring focus and precision, but prefers to avoid group activities because of social anxiety. She's quiet in the classroom and often seems distracted – probably due to the sensory overwhelm of the classroom. She's always on time and her written homework is always well-presented though she sometimes misses the point of the exercise.

In focus: AuDHD

Historically, the diagnostic manuals used to diagnose neurodivergence prevented clinicians from diagnosing an individual with both ADHD and autism, as these were thought to be mutually exclusive.

Since changes in 2013 that now permit a dual diagnosis, the co-occurrence rate of autism and ADHD appears to be somewhere around 75%.

A new, informal term, 'AuDHD', has evolved to describe this dual profile, which includes unique overlapping and sometimes competing autistic and ADHD traits (for example, a need for sameness and predictability paired with a difficulty with planning and organisation).

Dyslexia

What it is

Dyslexia is a developmental neurodivergence that primarily influences reading, writing, and spelling. Because of this, it's often classified as a *specific learning disability*. It's characterised by differences in processing written language, which can make tasks like decoding words, spelling accurately, or reading fluently more challenging. Dyslexia is not related to intelligence. Instead, it reflects unique ways the brain processes language.

In the public eye: Steve Jobs, co-founder of Apple Inc.

Prevalence

Estimates suggest that up to 10% of the population have some degree of dyslexia, making it one of the most common neurodivergences. Like other developmental differences, dyslexia is lifelong and varies in its impact from person to person.

Strengths

People with dyslexia often excel at big-picture thinking and oral skills, showing creativity in problem-solving and innovative approaches to tasks. Strong visual-spatial abilities are common, helping with interpreting complex diagrams, understanding 3D structures, or thinking in images. Many dyslexic individuals demonstrate entrepreneurial spirit and innovative thinking, bringing fresh ideas and perspectives to their fields.

Challenges

Dyslexia can make reading and writing slower and more effortful, leading to difficulties with spelling, decoding unfamiliar words and following text-heavy materials. Fast-paced reading or timed tasks may cause stress, and learners might avoid reading aloud or written work due to embarrassment or anxiety. Directions or instructions presented only in written form can be confusing.

Example student

Vik always brings a bubbly presence to the class. Their project work is always beautifully presented and often demonstrates some quite novel thinking about the task at hand. They excel in presentations but they often muddle false friends and their spelling and writing – when they eventually commit to a written task – can seem like it belongs to someone from a lower English level.

In focus: Is it dyslexia or Irlen Syndrome?

Irlen Syndrome is a lesser-known, light-based, visual-processing difference that anyone can have, but is more common among neurodivergent individuals. In fact, it's thought that around half of people with dyslexia and a third of those with ADHD may also have Irlen Syndrome.

Irlen Syndrome is a form a visual stress, affecting how well an individual can perceive detail in certain light. This often looks like difficulties with reading comprehension, line tracking and spelling, as well as fatigue and concentration difficulties.

Spectral filters (coloured lenses) in glasses can often resolve the visual stress and the specific colours required will vary from individual to individual. These are usually prescribed when someone receives an Irlen Syndrome diagnosis. Coloured overlays on printed text will also help. When learners appear to be struggling with reading, consider offering a range of coloured overlays for them to experiment with.

Dyspraxia (Developmental Coordination Disorder (DCD))

What it is

Dyspraxia (sometimes referred to as DCD), is a developmental neurodivergence that affects motor coordination, spatial awareness, balance and the organisation of movement. It involves difficulties with planning and executing physical tasks as well as difficulties with fine motor activities (for example, tying shoelaces), navigating physical spaces and following sequences of instructions.

In the public eye: Daniel Radcliffe, the actor famous for playing Harry Potter.

Prevalence

Estimates suggest that between 6% and 10% of people experience mild forms of dyspraxia, with around 2% experiencing more significant challenges. It's a lifelong and manifests in different ways for each individual.

Strengths

People with dyspraxia often show strong verbal communication skills and creativity. They may have heightened empathy and emotional insight, which can enrich social interactions and group work. Many develop excellent problem-solving abilities and persistence as they find unique ways to adapt and overcome physical challenges.

Challenges

Dyspraxia can make fine motor tasks like handwriting or typing more difficult and time-consuming. Organising materials, following sequences of instructions, or managing time efficiently might also present challenges. Physical clumsiness or balance difficulties may affect participation in some activities, and the extra effort required can lead to fatigue.

Example student

Ren contributes creatively to discussions and on group projects, and they often support weaker learners in the group by involving them in activities. They are often one of the last to arrive – sometimes late – and the last to pack up and leave as it seems to take them more time to put their things away. Timed tests cause them a lot of anxiety, but when left to prepare work at home on their laptop, they do really well.

Tourette's Syndrome and tic disorders

What it is

Tourette's Syndrome is a developmental neurodivergence that is characterised by involuntary movements and sounds called *tics*. Tics can be physical (such as blinking or shoulder shrugging) or vocal (such as throat clearing or grunting). Despite common misconceptions, swearing (known as *coprolalia*) is rare, affecting only about 10% of people with Tourette's. Tics can sometimes be controlled temporarily but require significant effort, which can be tiring.

In the public eye: award-winning musical artist Billie Eilish.

Prevalence

Around 1 in 100 people are thought to have Tourette's or a related tic condition. Many individuals develop coping strategies that help them manage symptoms, so tics might not always be apparent.

Strengths

People with Tourette's often develop strong focus and quick thinking, especially in high-pressure situations. Creativity and artistic talents are common, as is empathy and strong interpersonal skills, likely developed through managing social challenges related to tics.

Challenges

Inhibition difficulties can make formal classroom settings stressful. Managing tics requires concentration, which can be exhausting and impact participation. Misunderstandings or stigma around tics may cause anxiety or social isolation.

Example student

It took Isabel some time to come out of her shell, but now she is comfortable in the classroom, she has demonstrated that she can be an excellent storyteller and verbal communicator. She enjoys creative opportunities to use her English – including filming short video presentations – but in the classroom she often needs to pause mid-flow to regather herself. She sometimes spends a lot of a lesson coughing. Other times she seems too tired to participate or maintain concentration.

PTSD (Post-Traumatic Stress Disorder)

PTSD is unique in terms of its inclusion in this book – hence adding it here at the end. While the above are all forms of developmental neurodivergence, PTSD is something that is often included under the umbrella of acquired neurodivergence. However, I felt it was important to include PTSD for reasons I hope will become clear.

Trauma is an emotional and physiological response to deeply distressing or threatening events. Many people experience traumatic events in their lifetime but do not experience lasting effects. However, others will develop symptoms that persist for months or years after the event. PTSD affects not only a person's mood and behaviour, but also their cognition – hence its inclusion as a form of acquired neurodivergence. Common symptoms include irritability, restlessness, impulsivity, heightened startle responses, distractibility, low mood, sleep problems and memory issues.

Research shows us that neurodivergent people – particularly autistic individuals and those with ADHD – are significantly more likely to develop PTSD. People with ADHD, for example, are estimated to be four times more likely to develop PTSD than the neurotypical population.[19] Autistic individuals are thought to be around ten times more likely.[20] In addition, we also know that autistic people, people with ADHD, and disabled people more generally (including those with specific learning disabilities) are more likely to experience interpersonal victimisation, which may partly

---

19 Spencer, A. E., Faraone, S. V., Bogucki, O. E., Pope, A. L., Uchida, M., Milad, M. R., Spencer, T. J., Woodworth, K. Y., & Biederman, J. (2016) Examining the association between posttraumatic stress disorder and attention-deficit/hyperactivity disorder: a systematic review and meta-analysis. *The Journal of Clinical Psychiatry*, 77(1), 72–83. https://doi.org/10.4088/JCP.14r09479

20 Rumball, F., Brook, L., Happé, F. & Karl, A. (2021) Heightened risk of posttraumatic stress disorder in adults with autism spectrum disorder: The role of cumulative trauma and memory deficits. *Research in Developmental Disabilities*, 110, p.103848.

explain these elevated rates. Emerging studies now also suggest that neurodivergent people may have a heightened predisposition towards anxiety and trauma responses.[21, 22, 23, 24]

In practice, this means that some neurodivergent learners in your classroom may also be living with co-occurring PTSD, adding a further barrier to learning and engaging. In addition, in the international English language classroom there may be learners – with or without developmental neurodivergences – who have experienced adverse life circumstances such as poverty, insecure housing, forced migration, sexual violence, gang violence, civil unrest or war. These experiences may or may not be immediately visible to you.

The effects of PTSD can directly impact learners' abilities to engage in language learning tasks. Difficulties with attention, impulse control and memory may make it harder to follow instructions, stay focused during activities, or retain new vocabulary and grammar. Restlessness and heightened startle responses can interfere with classroom participation and increase anxiety. Recognising that some learners may be navigating these additional challenges alongside neurodivergence can help teachers create more supportive, flexible learning environments that reduce barriers and foster success.

---

21 Griffiths, S., Allison, C., Kenny, R., Holt, R., Smith, P., & Baron Cohen, S. (2019) The Vulnerability Experiences Quotient (VEQ): A study of vulnerability, mental health and life satisfaction in autistic adults. *Autism Research*, 12(10), 1516–1528. https://doi.org/10.1002/aur.2162

22 Office for National Statistics (ONS) (2019) *Disability and crime, UK: 2019* [online]. Available at: www.ons.gov.uk/peoplepopulationandcommunity/healthandsocialcare/disability/bulletins/disabilityandcrimeuk/2019 (accessed January 2026).

23 Merscher, J., Barra, S., Xander, A.M., Patrasc, P.G., Retz-Junginger, P. & Retz, W. (2025) Adult ADHD predicts intimate partner violence perpetration and victimization irrespective of gender and age. *Scientific Reports*, 15(1), p.4914.

24 Kampoureli, C.N., Rae, C.L., Van Praag, C.G., Harrison, N.A., Garfinkel, S.N., Critchley, H.D. & Eccles, J.A. (2025) Neural processes linking joint hypermobility and anxiety: key roles for the amygdala and insular cortex. *The British Journal of Psychiatry*, pp.1-7.

In focus: Trauma-informed practice

Originally developed within psychotherapeutic fields, the idea of *trauma-informed practice* offers a framework for adapting services to meet the unique needs of people who have experienced trauma and to avoid re-traumatisation.[25]

The focus in trauma-informed practice is on expanding the service-provider's empathy while also fostering a sense of safety.

The UK Government's Office for Health Improvement and Disparities has produced a free guidance note offering a working definition of trauma-informed practice.[26] It sets out six key principles that can be readily adapted to the language classroom:

1. **Safety:** Physical, psychological and emotional safety must be prioritised. Safeguarding policies should be in place, and learners should feel able to ask for what they need to feel safe. This might include adjustments to seating arrangements, options for opting out of certain activities, or agreed signals for taking breaks.
2. **Trustworthiness:** Transparency in policies and procedures is vital. Expectations should be clearly set without overpromising. In the classroom, this could mean explaining the purpose of activities, sticking to agreed schedules, and following through on commitments to build a climate of reliability.
3. **Choice:** Learners should be provided with opportunities to exercise autonomy, including in decision-making, topic selection and goal setting. Even small options, such as choosing between different tasks or how to present work, can help learners feel more in control of their learning experience.

25 Harris, M.E. & Fallot, R.D. (2001) *Using Trauma Theory to Design Service Systems.* Jossey-Bass/Wiley.

26 Office for Health Improvement and Disparities (OHID) (2022) *Working definition of trauma-informed practice* [online]. Available at: www.gov.uk/government/publications/working-definition-of-trauma-informed-practice (accessed January 2026).

4. **Collaboration:** Foster a culture of collaboration and peer support. This means encouraging learners to work together, share ideas and actively participate in shaping classroom activities. Collaboration between teacher and learners, such as co-creating class rules, can also enhance engagement and ownership.
5. **Empowerment:** Power should be shared with learners, giving them a strong voice in decisions that affect their learning. This involves listening to what they want and need, validating their feelings, and supporting them to take action. It also means recognising that those who have experienced trauma may feel powerless or isolated, or that they may lack self-worth, and actively working to counter this by fostering agency and celebrating achievements.
6. **Cultural consideration:** Move beyond stereotypes and biases linked to gender, sexual orientation, age, religion, disability, geography, race or ethnicity. Value and draw on learners' cultural knowledge, offer inclusive and responsive teaching, and design classroom practices and materials that reflect and respect the diversity of the learning community.

Further kinds of neurodivergence

There are many further kinds of neurodivergence, both developmental and acquired. This chapter has focused on some of most common minority neurotypes, but others you may encounter include:

- **Aphantasia:** A developmental neurodivergence that reduces a person's ability create mental images, even when trying to picture something familiar. This can affect how they recall memories, plan ahead or imagine scenarios, though many develop alternative ways≈of processing information, such as focusing on verbal or factual details instead. In the classroom, this may present as a difficulty with tasks that require visualising scenes or scenarios, or recalling visual images.
- **Developmental Language Disorder (DLD):** A neurodevelopmental condition that affects a person's ability to understand and/or use spoken language, without an obvious cause such as hearing loss or

intellectual disability. DLD can affect vocabulary, grammar, sentence structure and the ability to follow complex instructions. In the classroom, this may look like a difficulty following oral instructions.

- **Dysgraphia:** A developmental neurodivergence that affects a person's ability to plan, form and organise written language. In the classroom, this may show up as written text that's hard to read with inconsistent spelling.
- **Dyscalculia:** A developmental neurodivergence that affects a person's ability to understand, learn and work with numbers. In the classroom, this manifest as a hesitancy or anxiety around tasks that involve numbers or talking about money.
- **Pathological Demand Avoidance (PDA):** A profile that is often associated with autism, that involves an extreme avoidance of everyday demands and expectations. People with PDA experience high anxiety around feeling controlled or pressured, leading them to resist or evade demands in ways that are sometimes judged as challenging or oppositional. Some in the PDA self-advocate community prefer the name *Pervasive Drive for Autonomy*. In the classroom, this may look like severe anxiety or push-back in response to strict deadlines.

Common neurodivergent threads

While each minority neurotype presents in unique ways, there are certain characteristics that are consistent across many different forms of neurodivergence, including differences in communication, sensory processing and executive functioning. These can be strengths in some contexts and challenges in others, and they may sometimes overlap with or be compounded by experiences like PTSD. Recognising these shared patterns helps us move beyond labels and instead focus on creating flexible, learner-responsive environments that reduce barriers and support participation: we'll look at this in more depth in Section Two.

Many neurodivergent individuals, for example, experience differences in *executive functioning* – the mental processes that help us plan, organise, initiate and complete tasks. These differences might show up as difficulties with time management, task-switching, remembering instructions or staying focused in busy classroom settings. Rather than signalling laziness or disengagement, these can be signs that learners may need additional scaffolding or different ways of accessing and demonstrating their learning

Sensory differences also cut across a number of minority neurotypes. Some learners may be hypersensitive to sounds, lights, smells or textures, to the extent that their ability to engage with activities may be seriously reduced. Others may be hyposensitive (under-sensitive) and seek out additional sensory input (for example, in the form of *stimming* (see below)). Whatever the unique sensory profile of a neurodivergent learner, the sensory environment of the classroom can significantly affect their comfort and concentration. Sensory details that may appear minor – from background noise and lighting to seating and visual clutter – can have major impacts.

Aa Terminology note: Stimming

Stimming is the name given to the repetitive actions or movements that neurodivergent people often use to regulate their emotions or to manage sensory input.

These can vary in type, frequency and intensity, but all serve a similar purpose: to self-soothe and self-regulate. As such, they are an important part of neurodivergent wellbeing and wherever possible should be supported.

Stimming might look like: chewing gum, twirling hair, clicking a pen, foot-tapping, humming, rocking on a chair, feeling certain textures between their fingers or on their face, jumping, clicking their fingers, swaying, clicking their tongue, crunching on crisps, waving a pen before their eyes, spinning a fidget tool… and an infinite number of alternatives!

Another common thread is that being neurodivergent in a world oriented towards neurotypical norms and needs can be an uncomfortable or stressful experience. Many neurodivergent people, as a consequence, develop anxiety, chronic stress, depression or self-blame. In addition to this, neurodivergent people are more predisposed to developing more generalised anxiety than the neurotypical population. In the classroom, this may show up as a hesitancy to contribute in group activities, perfectionism, performance pressure or lack of confidence.

What is vital to keep in mind, is that there is no single template for neurodivergence overall, nor for any individual neurodivergent profile. No two autistic students will have the same sensory profile. Learners with ADHD won't all struggle with time. Handwriting won't be difficult for every dyspraxic student. That's why flexibility in our teaching approach is so important. Rather than trying to second-guess every possible individual need, we can prepare lessons that offer multiple ways to access, process and produce language. This allows us to shift the question from 'What is it about this student that means they can't learn?' to 'How can we design more supportive and inclusive learning environments for all?' In Section Two we'll look more closely at something called *Universal Design for Learning* which aims to do just this, as well as ways to bring this into the English language classroom.

TL:DR (too long: didn't read) summary

- There are many different types of neurodivergence. The most common minority neurotypes you might expect to encounter in the classroom include ADHD, autism, dyslexia, dyspraxia, Tourette's and PTSD.
- ADHD affects attention regulation, impulse control and activity levels, presenting in inattentive, hyperactive-impulsive, or combined types. ADHD often includes creativity and hyperfocus alongside challenges with organisation and sustained attention.
- Autism is a diverse, lifelong neurodivergence influencing communication, information processing and sensory processing. Autistic strengths include detail focus, memory and unique perspectives alongside challenges with sensory sensitivities and social anxiety.
- Dyslexia primarily impacts reading, writing and spelling. Many dyslexic learners excel at big-picture thinking, creativity and oral skills.

- Dyspraxia affects motor coordination and spatial awareness. People with dyspraxia often possess strong verbal and problem-solving skills, but can experience difficulties with fine motor tasks, balance and organisation.
- Tourette's involves involuntary tics that can be vocal or physical. Many people with Tourette's excel in creativity and tasks requiring a strong focus, despite social challenges related to stigma and symptom management.
- PTSD, as an acquired neurodivergence, is often more prevalent among neurodivergent individuals. Learners with PTSD may experience difficulties with attention, impulse control and severe anxiety in the classroom.
- Common threads across neurodivergences include differences in executive functioning, sensory processing and increased risk of anxiety, highlighting the need for flexible, inclusive teaching approaches that focus on learners' strengths and reducing barriers.

Reflective questions

1. Which of these neurotypes have you encountered in your teaching so far? Knowing what you do now, would you have done anything differently?
2. How does your current teaching practice already support some of these learners?
3. Where might you need to rethink common assumptions about attention, participation or ability?
4. How could you offer more than one route to success in a lesson or assessment?
5. What kinds of flexibility could benefit multiple learners, not just those with formal diagnoses?

Section Two

Neurodiverse Classrooms

Chapter 3: Inclusion and neurodivergent learners: our responsibilities

By the end of this chapter you'll be able to:

- define meaningful 'inclusion'
- describe some of the key legislation in relation to disability and neurodiversity inclusion
- recognise your responsibilities for inclusive teaching
- assess how inclusive your teaching currently is and identify areas for improvement.

In Section One of this book, we explored what neurodiversity means, how different models of disability shape our understanding of it, and the wide range of neurodivergent profiles that might be present in any learning space. Armed with this understanding, in Section Two we're now shifting our focus from ideas to implications and thinking about neurodiversity in the classroom.

In this chapter, we'll explore our legal and ethical responsibilities towards neurodivergent learners. We'll look at inclusion as a fundamental right for every student and consider where the responsibility for making this a reality truly lies; whether with individual teachers, educational institutions, or the wider governing bodies that shape policy and practice. In the next chapter, we'll move from theory to practice and explore a practical framework (Universal Design for Learning) that can help make inclusion achievable in everyday teaching.

Before we delve any deeper into our responsibilities as educators, I'd like to first share with you an experience from early in my teaching career that I've replayed in my mind many times over the years. It's a small vignette, but one that perhaps speaks to a larger truth – that teachers often carry the weight of inclusion, but meaningful accessibility also requires support, resources and awareness at an institutional level. Even well-intentioned teachers can struggle when those structures aren't in place. Throughout this section and the rest of the book, we'll consider how we can best equip ourselves to make our teaching as accessible and equitable as possible, but for now, let's travel back nearly 20 years in time…

Evening ESOL Entry 1 class

One of my earliest teaching posts, not long out of my CELTA training, was as an ESOL (English for Speakers of Other Languages) lecturer at a local community college.

My Thursday evening class was an Entry Level 1 group – i.e. complete beginners. Some of the learners were migrant workers from Eastern Europe who had come to England to try and make a living, often working all hours to send money to their families back home and squeezing their English lessons around a packed schedule. Others were members of the local 'settled community' — in my group, this mostly included older Bangladeshi women whose husbands were local small business owners and who (now that their children were growing up) were taking the opportunity to learn English for themselves. We also had a small number of teenage asylum seekers in the group: very young men who had fled from the conflict in Afghanistan. Already, there were a lot of different needs in the room that needed careful balancing and minimal shared language resources to work with.
I quickly fell absolutely in love with this warm and hard-working group,

and it warmed my heart every time I saw a flash of joy or pride flicker across a learner's face as a new piece of language locked in. For these learners, starting right at the beginning: *every single word mattered.* They were already here, in England, living their lives through English, and these evenings once a week when we found ourselves in a room together helped them have more autonomy and agency in their everyday interactions: to have more of a voice.

One of the students in this class was a young Polish man, who was profoundly Deaf. I discovered this on day one as we went through the register. For the first few sessions, a sign language interpreter would arrive to help support him, usually dashing in a minute or two after we'd begun as, being a freelancer, they were coming directly from other work elsewhere. On some weeks when his main interpreter couldn't make it, a supply interpreter would turn up in their place – seemingly not knowing anything about the learner or the class. Sometimes, no supply interpreter was found in time. Because it was the evening (and therefore out of office hours), there was no one I could call even if I'd been able to leave the group on their own to walk down the long college corridor to use the staffroom phone.

There was already a lot of exaggerated gesticulation in my teaching of this Beginner group, but in these evenings I'd ramp up the miming and clowning further: if nothing else, it often elicited laughter that brought us all together, this learner included. I'd make sure he could see my mouth whenever I was speaking to the class, and I tried my best to add in British Sign Language fingerspelling for key words... It's all I felt able to do.

But packing up after everyone had left and reflecting on the fact that British Sign Language (BSL) – the language of not only my fingerspelling but also of the interpreter – is a completely different language to Polish Sign Language (Polski Język Migowy (PJM)), an uncomfortable nagging feeling would grow inside.

This was a poor setup – that was clear to me – but at the time, as a relatively new teacher, I didn't feel resourced or informed enough to handle it any better...

How does this vignette relate to neurodiversity in English language teaching, you may be asking yourself? For me, the connections lie in the (in this case, missed) opportunities for making learning accessible to individuals with disabilities and divergent needs. The Deaf learner in this account wasn't effectively included in the learning activities at all times, and as a consequence he was, ultimately, partially excluded. It wasn't his Deafness that led to his exclusion: it was the failure to properly accommodate his needs.

Where the responsibility lies for this failing is complex. As the teacher, I felt a lot of guilt and inadequacy for not being able to include him fully at all times. Yet, as a newly qualified, hourly-paid lecturer, there were limitations in what I was able to deliver. As a department, there could have perhaps been more support or training around disability inclusion, but with existing high demands on resources, tight budget restrictions and limited discourse within the profession (at the time) around disability in the classroom, I can see why it wasn't a top priority. As a large, multi-departmental community college, you might expect internal policy around diversity, equity and inclusion, but without clearly defined benchmarking standards for how inclusion looks in practice, it's easy for delivery to fall short.

In this instance, the learner's support needs were evident yet not fully met. For many neurodivergent learners, support needs may be less apparent and less easily recognised. This challenge – understanding what inclusion really involves – is one we'll return to throughout the rest of this section. But first, let's take a moment to consider what *inclusion* really means.

Inclusion: What is does it mean?

In most institutions, there will now be policy – or even whole departments – dedicated to DEI, where D stands for *diversity*, E for *equity* and I for *inclusion*. A further letter is sometimes added to the acronym: B for *belonging*. DEI(B) frameworks have the shared aim of establishing fair treatment and equitable access to services or public spaces, especially for those who have experienced marginalisation or discrimination based on identity or disability.

Diversity addresses the importance of ensuring the presence of different people with difference experiences and perspectives. *Equity* highlights the importance of fairness in opportunities, access and support – and the use of 'equity' here (rather than 'equality') is important. With *equality*, everybody is treated equally and given equal supports.[27] Some people will not need these supports, and for others these supports will be inadequate. With *equity*, individuals are provided with unique supports that match their specific needs, enabling equal access for all.[28] Finally, *inclusion* speaks to the need to meaningfully involve these diverse perspectives in a way that promotes autonomy and allows everyone's voices to be heard.

Inclusion in English language teaching

In the context of English language teaching, inclusion means ensuring that all learners can participate fully and meaningfully in learning activities, regardless of background, ability or neurotype. In their *Continuing Professional Development Framework for Teachers*, the British Council defines inclusive practice as identifying, understanding, and addressing the diversity of learners and their needs:

> *'This includes identifying the barriers and challenges that marginalised learners face, understanding the pedagogical strategies that impact learner outcomes, addressing the diversity of learners during the teaching and learning processes, and demonstrating and encouraging inclusive behaviour in and outside the classroom.'*[29]

This approach aligns with the social model of disability, introduced earlier in this book. From this perspective, we understand that barriers to participation result from disabling environments and systems, not from the individual's disability or difference. Applying this model in language teaching directs our attention away from thinking about what we may believe a learner can't do, or appears to struggle with, and instead towards what it might be about the learning context that is limiting this learner's access.

---

27 There is a very good infographic, which I won't try to recreate with my poor drawing skills, but you can find easily by searching 'equality versus equity' online. It illustrates the difference between equality and equity, based on people trying to watch a baseball game over a fence.

28 There is, of course, a third option, whereby systemic barriers are removed, meaning no additional supports are needed. This is an idyll that that *Universal Design for Learning* – the focus of our next chapter – tries to move us toward.

29 British Council (2025) *Teaching for Success: Continuing Professional Development (CPD) Framework for teachers* [online]. Available at: www.teachingenglish.org.uk/sites/teacheng/files/2025-04/CPD%20Framework%20for%20teachers%202025%20-%20Guidance%20Booklet.pdf (accessed January 2026).

Legislation and governance

Promoting accessibility in the classroom and providing reasonable adjustments is not simply an ethical responsibility for educators: it is also mandated by international and national legislation, policies and governance frameworks. One key international instrument that establishes these rights and obligations is the United Nations Convention on the Rights of Persons with Disabilities (CRPD), which provides a global standard for accessibility and inclusion.

Terminology note: *Talking about disability*

As language teachers, we're especially attuned to how powerful words can be. When it comes to talking about disability, different terminology can carry different meanings and associations that shape how individuals feel about themselves and how they feel others see them.

- **Person-first language** (for example, 'a person with a disability'). This way of talking about disability emerged in the 1970s from the disability rights movement in the Global North. The aim was to foreground the personhood of the individual in an attempt to counter the perceived dehumanisation of the language of the medical model of disability. Some people with disabilities still prefer this structure and it is more dominant in American English.
- **Identity-first language** (for example, 'a disabled person'). This way of talking about disability emerged as a reaction to person-first language in certain disabled communities, especially outside of the USA. Identity-first language aligns itself with the social model of disability by linguistically framing disability as something that *happens* to a person (by external factors, for example, a disabling environment). This structure is more commonly preferred by neurodivergent individuals, but this varies between individuals and more granular neurodivergent identities (for example, between autistic people and people with ADHD).
- For some disabilities, when there is a strong sense of a cultural or community identity, terms are usually capitalised in English. Most notably you will find this for Deaf and Deaf-blind people, although there is also growing use of it among the autistic community, and others, too.

- **Learning disability vs intellectual disability.** There is sometimes confusion around these terms, not helped by the fact that they are used differently in American and British English. In British English, people who require additional support to learn, make decisions and manage daily life (compared with what is typical for their age) are described (and describe themselves) as having a 'learning disability'. But take note – the term 'specific learning disability' (SLD) will usually refer to a developmental difference in a specific area of learning or behaviour such as dyslexia, dyscalculia or dyspraxia. In American English, the term 'intellectual disability' is used instead. In British English, 'intellectual disability' can sometimes be seen as quite stigmatising.

As with all person-centred approaches, take the lead from individual learners themselves about how they identify and prefer to describe themselves.

International rights

The United Nations (UN) Convention on the Rights of Persons with Disabilities (CRPD), adopted in December 2006, was the first human rights treaty to directly involve stakeholders (i.e. disabled individuals) in its negotiation and development.[30] Adopting a social model of disability perspective, the CRPD outlines essential rights of citizens of member states with 'long-term physical, mental, intellectual or sensory impairments which in interaction with various barriers may hinder their full and effective participation in society on an equal basis with others' (Article 1, CRPD). As of April 2025, all 193 UN member states have ratified the CRPD, meaning that they are legally bound to abide by its provisions.

Article 24 of the CRPD defines how those rights apply specifically to education, establishing the international right to education 'without discrimination and on the basis of equal opportunity for all learners'. Inclusivity and accessibility are enshrined in this Article, in part through the commitment to provide 'reasonable accommodation' of disability-related, individual learner needs.

30 United Nations (2006) *Convention on the Rights of Persons with Disabilities*. New York, 13 December 2006, Treaty Series, vol. 2515, p. 3. Available at: https://social.desa.un.org/issues/disability/crpd/convention-on-the-rights-of-persons-with-disabilities-crpd (accessed January 2026).

In focus: 'Accommodations' or 'Reasonable Adjustments'

Disabled learners in UN member states are legally entitled to reasonable adjustments (sometimes called 'accommodations') that enable them to access education on an equitable basis with others. These may include adaptations to teaching, learning environments or additional supports that help to remove barriers to participation. What counts as a *reasonable* adjustment depends on its relevance and effectiveness, balanced against the practicality and cost of putting it in place.

Potential reasonable adjustments for teaching and learning include:

- changing the physical location of a class
- providing alternative forms of in-class communication
- enlarging print or printing on differently coloured paper
- providing materials in sign, or in an alternative format
- providing students with a note-taker or supporting the use of digital note-taking tools
- allowing students to use assistive technology in learning and assessment situations
- allowing a student additional time
- reducing levels of background noise to help manage sensory overload
- providing alternative evaluation methods or replacing an element of curriculum with an alternative element.

(Adapted from UNICEF- 'Inclusive Education'[31])

Note of caution: Reasonable adjustments are vital for inclusion, yet they are not infallible. They rely on learners recognising and communicating their own needs, which is something not all learners are able, confident, or informed enough to do – especially in a second (or third, or fourth language).

31 UNICEF (2017) *Inclusive Education: Understanding Article 24 of the Convention on the Rights of Persons with Disabilities* [online]. Available at: www.unicef.org/eca/sites/unicef.org.eca/files/IE_summary_accessible_220917_0.pdf (accessed January 2026).

National rights

While the CRPD sets out international standards, many countries will have their own national laws and policies that locally define the rights of disabled people and the responsibilities of educational providers.

In the UK, for example – my own teaching context – we have *the* UK Equality Act (2010), which legally protects people from discrimination in education, employment and wider society on the basis of nine protected characteristics, including disability.[32] The Equality Act continues the emphasis from the CRPD that it is the responsibility of education providers to make *reasonable adjustments* to their delivery to ensure disabled learners are not placed at a substantial disadvantage compared with their peers.

It is perhaps worth noting that neurodivergence itself is not a named, protected characteristic. However, disability is defined within this act as a person with 'a physical or mental impairment' which 'has a substantial and long-term adverse effect on [their] ability to carry out normal day-to-day activities'. The slightly pathologising language aside, we can see that neurodivergence(s) would be defined in this way.

Across the world, there are many parallel laws. In the USA, for example, the Americans with Disabilities Act (1990)[33] and the Individuals with Disabilities Education Act (IDEA)[34] establish clear rights to accessible education. In Japan, the Act for Eliminating Discrimination against Persons with Disabilities (2013) requires 'reasonable accommodation' in schools and other public services.[35] In the United Arab Emirates, Federal Law No. 29 of 2006 guarantees equal educational opportunities and requires that institutions make necessary adaptations, including the use of sign language, Braille, or other accessible communication methods.[36]

---

32 *Equality Act* (2010) UK: www.legislation.gov.uk/ukpga/2010/15/contents (accessed January 2026).

33 United States Congress (1990) *Americans with Disabilities Act of 1990*, Pub. L. No. 101-336, 104 Stat. 327. (Amended by the ADA Amendments Act of 2008, Pub. L. No. 110-325, 122 Stat. 3553). Av

34 United States Congress (2004) *Individuals with Disabilities Education Improvement Act of 2004*, Pub. L. No. 108-446, 118 Stat. 2647. (Originally enacted as the Education for All Handicapped Children Act, 1975, Pub. L. No. 94-142.)

35 *Act for Eliminating Discrimination against Persons with Disabilities*, Japan. (Act No. 65 of June 26, 2013). Available online at: www.japaneselawtranslation.go.jp/en/laws/view/4930/ (accessed January 2026).

36 *Federal Law No. 29 of 2006 Concerning the Rights of Persons with Special Needs*, United Arab Emirates. Available at: www.mohesr.gov.ae/En/Legislation/Pages/default.aspx (accessed January 2026).

The details may differ very slightly depending on where you teach, but in almost all places around the world, inclusion is not only an ethical responsibility, but a legal one, too.

As a quick fact-finding task about local legislation, see if you can find the answers to the following questions:

- What national legislation is there in the country of your current teaching context that addresses accessibility and disability rights? If you've taught in other countries, what was the legislation there?
- What governmental or professional agencies have oversight for this in the context of education?
- What are the consequences if organisations or education providers breach their duties for inclusion?

Neurodivergent rights

Most recently for educators within the European Union, new legislation was introduced in mid-2025 that has a direct bearing on neurodivergence in the classroom. The new European Accessibility Act (EAA) sets out common accessibility standards for products and services across all EU member states.[37] Crucially, these standards explicitly include the accessibility needs of neurodivergent learners, meaning that teachers, schools and educational institutions are legally required to consider and accommodate a wide range of cognitive, sensory and learning differences.

Governance within English language teaching

Because English language teaching takes place in such a diversity of contexts and countries, there is no single body overseeing professional standards worldwide. However, we can look to respected, international ELT organisations to identify common priorities and areas of focus for teachers.

For example, in the British Council's recent phased review of its Continuing Professional Development (CPD2) Framework, a large survey of EFL teachers found that 'being inclusive of all learners' was considered one of the most important areas for professional growth, tied with 'giving

37 European Commission (2025) *European Accessibility Act*. Available at: https://commission.europa.eu/strategy-and-policy/policies/justice-and-fundamental-rights/disability/union-equality-strategy-rights-persons-disabilities-2021-2030/european-accessibility-act_en (accessed January 2026).

formative feedback'.[38] Here, an enormous 99% of participants agreed that inclusive practice was a key priority for their ongoing development. Similarly, TESOL International Association's TESOL DEIA (Diversity, Equity, Inclusion, and Access) Initiative, launched in 2021, demonstrates a refocusing on inclusive practice in ELT.[39]

This emphasis by leading ELT organisations on foregrounding inclusion in the ELT classroom aligns with the legislative frameworks discussed above, and a growing public understanding about diversity and individual learner needs. They also underscore the importance of professional development in equipping educators to meet these diverse (and *divergent*) needs.

Reflecting on your own practice

Hopefully by now you'll have a clearer sense of the practical meaning of disability and neurodiversity inclusion in the classroom, and an idea of which governance frameworks apply in your teaching context. In the next chapter, we'll look in more detail at Universal Design for Learning – an educational approach that aims to make inclusion more achievable. First, why not take a moment to reflect on how inclusive your current teaching practices are? You might surprise yourself!

At the end of this book, you'll find a series of Appendices featuring various reflective tools and resources. The first of these (page 145 – 'Inclusive learning self-evaluative tool') is an audit framework that can support your self-evaluation of inclusivity in your current teaching practices. This tool has been adapted from a larger resource, developed by Mike Wray to assess inclusivity across Higher Education departments in the UK – but it also functions well for the ELT classroom.[40] In it, you will find three sections (Before Teaching, During Teaching and Assessment) with a number of statements in each that are indicative of good inclusive practice. Take a moment, before moving on the next chapter, to take stock of where you are right now. Read through the statements and rate

38 Motteram, G. & Dawson, S. (2025) What's changed in English Language Teaching? A review of change in the teaching and learning of English and in teacher education and development from 2014-2024. *British Council.* https://doi.org/10.57884/FPE8-5130

39 TESOL (2021) TESOL DEIA Initiative [online]. Available at: www.tesol.org/about/deia-initiative/ (accessed January 2026).

40 Wray, M. (2020) *Inclusive Learning, Teaching and Assessment Framework* [online]. York: York St John University. Available at: https://inclusioninhe.com/projects/iltaf/ (accessed January 2026).

yourself against each statement from 5 (I do this very well now) to 1 (I don't address this yet) and use what you identify as the basis for two or three key actions points – areas you would like to develop or steps you would like to take to increase inclusion.

Remember, if some of your present scores feel lower than you'd like, don't worry. None of us gets everything right straight away (I know this very well!), and inclusion comes from joint responsibility and collective action that we build over time. Simply taking the time to reflect on your practice in this way already demonstrates a genuine commitment and marks a meaningful step toward more inclusive teaching.

TL:DR (too long: didn't read) summary

- Inclusion is a both a right and a responsibility. Every learner has an ethical and legal right to be able to access education on an equitable basis, without facing discrimination.
- Inclusion means creating learning environments where every student can participate, contribute and thrive, by removing barriers and adapting environments rather than expecting learners to adapt to them.
- Teachers, institutions and governing bodies all share responsibility for making this a reality.
- International treaties such as the UN Convention on the Rights of Persons with Disabilities, and national legislation such as the UK's Equality Act, mandate inclusive practices within education, often requiring anticipatory 'reasonable adjustments' (or 'accommodations') for disabled learners.
- Reasonable adjustments remove barriers to participation and make learning accessible. These can include changes to teaching methods or learning environments, or the provision of additional supports. What counts as 'reasonable' is determined by how well it addresses the learner's needs in context balanced against practical and financial feasibility.

- There are different ways to talk about disability. Some individuals or disabled groups may prefer person-first language (such as 'a person with disability' or 'a person with dyspraxia'), whereas others may prefer identity-first language (such as 'a disabled person' or 'a Deaf person'). In different contexts, some terminology or language constructions can be experienced as stigmatising. As such, people can sometimes feel strongly about the language used to talk about their disability – always respect individual preferences.

Reflective questions

1. As a teacher, how do you currently identify if a student has disability or neurodiversity-related access needs? What are the strengths and weaknesses of this current system?
2. If students are expected to approach you themselves to highlight their access needs, what barriers can you anticipate? What small step could you take right now to help minimise those barriers?
3. Think of a time when a student's needs surprised you. How did you respond?

Chapter 4:
Universal Design for Learning

By the end of this chapter you'll be able to:

- contextualise the origins of Universal Design and Universal Design for Learning (UDL) within the disability rights movement
- explain the key principles of UDL
- describe the differences between UDL and traditional classroom differentiation
- reflect on how you can apply UDL to your EFL classroom practice.

English language teaching occurs in all manner of contexts, all around the world, from small living rooms to summer school classrooms, from large university lecture halls to remote digital platforms. It can be synchronous or asynchronous, delivered to fixed cohorts or to ever-changing groups with rolling-enrolment. When you add to this diversity of contexts the differing access needs of neurodivergent learners, the prospect of planning for neurodivergence can feel (understandably) overwhelming – especially when trying to make reasonable adjustments for multiple learners within a single lesson.

Thankfully, there is an approach that aims to minimise superfluous, individualised accommodations by making learning environments broadly accessible to all from the outset. In this chapter, we'll explore this framework – called Universal Design for Learning (UDL) – and learn how it seeks to empower teachers to pre-emptively remove barriers, thus reducing the need for extensive individual adjustments.

We'll begin by tracing the origins of UDL before moving on to consider its three key principles and their application in ELT settings. The chapter closes with a reflective self-audit tool that will help you evaluate your current teaching and pinpoint manageable but immediate changes you can make to ensure your lessons are more accessible for all learners.

Universal Design

The mid-20th century saw a lot of social changes begin to take place worldwide. Post-war societies suddenly found themselves needing to accommodate a large number of recently disabled veterans. Medical advancements meant that more children were surviving into adulthood, and adults were living longer, resulting in an increasingly ageing populations.

As campaigns for civil and human rights mounted over the following decades, the disability rights movement also found a voice in the early 1980s. In parallel with the popularisation of Mike Oliver's social model of disability[41] (which we encountered in Chapter 1), perspectives began to shift towards seeing disablement and exclusion as arising from the external environment rather than from the individual. Gradually, it became apparent that if appropriate accommodations and adjustments could be made to public spaces, transport and housing, people with all kinds of differing needs could experience more equitable access and inclusion within society.

It was against this backdrop that Ronald Mace, a disabled American architect, coined the term Universal Design in the 1980s. Universal Design is a design philosophy that rejects the common wisdom of designing for an 'average' user and instead aims to create environments and products that are usable by as many people as possible, regardless of age or ability. A working group of architects, product designers, engineers and environmental design researchers led by Mace and based

41 Oliver, M. (1983) *Social Work with Disabled People*. Practical Social Work Series, BASW.

at North Carolina State University (NCSU) developed these ideas into the seven core *Principles of Universal Design* that have been widely adopted in design standards worldwide.[42]

Principles of Universal Design[43]

1. **Equitable use:** The design is useful and marketable to people with diverse abilities.
2. **Flexibility in use:** The design accommodates a wide range of individual preferences and abilities.
3. **Simple and intuitive use:** The design is easy to understand, regardless of the user's experience, knowledge, language skills or current concentration level.
4. **Perceptible information:** The design communicates necessary information effectively to the user, regardless of ambient conditions or the user's sensory abilities.
5. **Tolerance for error:** The design minimises hazards and the adverse consequences of accidental or unintended actions.
6. **Low physical and cognitive effort:** The design can be used efficiently and comfortably and with minimum fatigue.
7. **Size and space for approach and use:** The design provides appropriate sizing and spacing of elements, allowing the user to interact successfully.

Many aspects of everyday design that we may now take for granted – such as dropped kerbs[44], ramps, lifts ('elevators' for the non-British readers among you), wide doors and low-floored buses – originated from Universal Design principles. As Universal Design ideas spread beyond architecture, educators began to explore how its principles could shape learning environments. Researchers such as Sheryl Burgstahler at the University of Washington advanced the concept of Universal Design

42 Story, M. F., Mueller, J. L., & Mace, R. L. (1998) *The Universal Design File: Designing for People of All Ages and Abilities*. Raleigh, NC: Center for Universal Design, North Carolina State University.

43 The Centre for Excellence in Universal Design (2025) *The 7 Principles* [online]. Available at: https://universaldesign.ie/about-universal-design/the-7-principles (accessed January 2026).

44 It was architect Selwyn Goldsmith, in the UK, who pioneered the first dropped kerbs in Norwich during the 1960s, following consultation with wheelchair users.

in Education (UDE)[45], while the Center for Applied Special Technology (CAST) in the US developed the framework known as Universal Design for Learning (UDL), applying the same inclusive design philosophy to teaching and curriculum design, and laying the foundations for more inclusive educational practice.

Universal Design for Learning (UDL)

Just as architecture and design began to move away from an 'average' intended user, so Universal Design for Learning moves us away from an imagined, average student. Continuing to draw on the social model of disability, UDL shifts the emphasis from the individual and their unique access needs, to the institution and the ways in which it can remove or minimise barriers to learning from the outset. Central to UDL is the understanding that all students are beginning from differing starting points: bringing different identities, learning preferences, needs, abilities and neurotypes to their learning experience.[46] In the introduction to their book exploring UDL in Higher Education settings, Martin, Wray and Krupa summarise this very well:

> 'In UDL terms there is no such person as Mythical Norm (i.e. the average student), and planning for diversity is at the core of the development of inclusive pedagogy and practices…'[47]

In focus: 'The mythical norm' – Audre Lorde

Whenever I give talks or training on neurodiversity, I always like to refer quite early on to the concept – coined by Audre Lorde – of the *mythical norm.*

Audre Lorde was a self-described 'Black, lesbian, feminist, socialist, mother, warrior, poet', as well as a professor, philosopher and civil

45 Burgstahler, S. E. (2009) *Universal Design in Education: Principles and applications.* Seattle, WA: DO-IT, University of Washington.

46 Al-Azawei, A., Serenelli, F. & Lundqvist, K. (2016) Universal Design for Learning (UDL): A content analysis of peer reviewed journals from 2012 to 2015. *Journal of the Scholarship of Teaching and Learning*, 16(3), pp.39-56.

47 Martin, N., Wray, M. & Krupa, J. (2025) *Universal Design for Learning: A critical approach.* London and New York: Routledge.

rights activist.[48] In a paper delivered at the Copeland Colloquium, Amherst College, in 1980, exploring how capitalist societies construct and enforce ideals of who holds power and who belongs, Lorde said:

> *'Much of Western European history conditions us to see human differences in simplistic opposition to each other: dominant/subordinate, good/bad, up/down, superior/inferior. In a society where the good is defined in terms of profit rather than in terms of human need, there must always be some group of people who, through systematised oppression, can be made to feel surplus, to occupy the place of the dehumanised inferior...*
>
> *'...Somewhere, on the edge of consciousness, there is what I call a mythical norm, which each one of us within our hearts knows "that is not me". In America, the norm is usually defined as white, thin, male, young, heterosexual, Christian, and financially secure. It is with this mythical norm that the trappings of power reside within this society.'*

For Lorde, although the mythical norm determines who is afforded power and who is marginalised, it is, in the end, simply a myth. None of us truly measure up to all of its demands, and certainly not sustainably – we can't stay young forever, for example.

In education, and particularly in ELT, this concept is especially relevant. Our classrooms are often inherently diverse – in languages, cultures, lived experiences and neurotypes. The mythical norm was never real, and neither is the 'average' English language learner.

UDL Guidelines: Three key principles

The Center for Applied Special Technology (CAST) is a nonprofit organisation focused on inclusive education. In the early 1990s, CAST developed the UDL Guidelines to help teachers design learning that works for all students, for both those with disabilities and without. The UDL Guidelines offer practical strategies to reduce barriers and support

48 This description is a widely cited verbal introduction to herself that Lorde often made at the start of her public talks. See: Poetry Foundation (web article, no date). *Audre Lorde: 1934—1992.* Available at: www.poetryfoundation.org/poets/audre-lorde (accessed January 2026).

diverse ways of learning, moving beyond the idea of an 'average' student or a mythical norm.[49] They serve as a living, evolving resource, continually updated to reflect new research, practice and insights from educators and learners, with the latest version updated in 2024. The guidelines are divided into three key principles, focusing on modes of *engagement*, *representation* and *action/expression*.

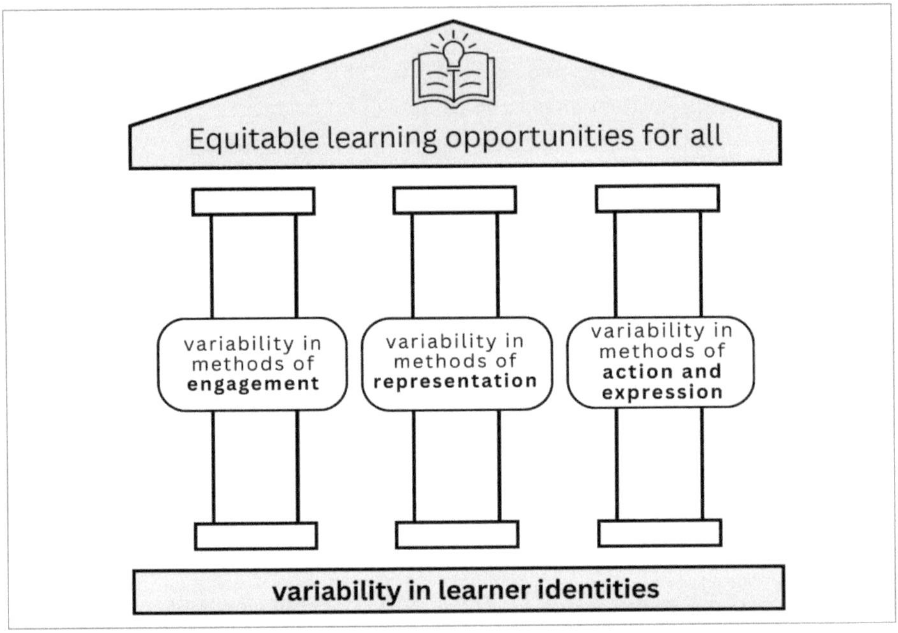

Figure 4.2: A black and white graphic image of a three-columned colonnade. In the 'roof' area, text reads 'equitable learning opportunities for all', below an icon showing an open book and a lightbulb. Over column one is text reading 'variability in methods of engagement'. Over column two is text reading 'variability in methods of representation'. Over column three is text reading 'variability in methods of action and expression'. Below, along the bottom, text reads 'variability in learner identities'.

UDL acknowledge that learners are all beginning from different places and bringing different experiences, skills and needs to bear on their learning. To make learning as accessible and inclusive as possible, it offers three pillars of universal adjustments that we can make to our teaching and assessment that aim to minimise the need for bespoke, individualised accommodations.[50]

49 Center for Applied Special Technology (CAST) (2024) *UDL Guidelines 3.0* [online]. Available at: https://udlguidelines.cast.org/more/about-guidelines-3-0/ (accessed January 2026).

50 N.B. The purpose of UDL is not to *remove* the need for accommodations and reasonable adjustments for individual learners. Some learners will still require additional and sometimes specialist supports (e.g. a Deaf learner may require a sign language interpreter).

While the concept of adjusting instruction to accommodate different learners may feel familiar to those who already use *differentiation* within their teaching, UDL is slightly different. It moves away from changing lessons for individual students and instead involves planning lessons in a way that makes them flexible and accessible for everyone from the very beginning. In ELT, differentiation often means making adjustments for particular learners based on our expert assessment of their learning needs. We might grade our language, vary the level of task scaffolding, adapt input or materials, or provide extension activities for faster finishers. UDL instead takes the approach of adapting lessons *before* identifying individual needs by building in flexibility from the outset.

Pillar one: Multiple means of engagement

The first pillar focuses on how we engage learners, highlighting the need to provide varied and flexible ways for students to connect with learning, sustain interest, and find personal relevance in what they study and in the wider student experience.

In practice, this may look like:

- allowing learners to choose topics for discussion or writing that relate to their interests or cultures
- using gamified activities, challenges or storytelling to sustain motivation
- providing options for collaborative and individual work depending on learners' preferences
- incorporating tasks that connect classroom language to wider student experiences (for example, campus life, work, hobbies, current events).

Pillar two: Multiple means of representation

This second pillar speaks to the need offer a variety of ways for students to access information and learning resources.

In practice, this may look like:

- providing learning materials in multiple formats: visual (charts, diagrams), auditory (recordings), and written
- offering texts at different reading levels or including summaries/glossaries

- presenting text materials in multiple versions (for example, with colour coding for different parts of speech) or on a variety of coloured paper to support readability
- using subtitles or printed transcripts for listening materials and videos
- supporting comprehension with graphic organisers, mind maps or annotated examples.

Pillar three: Design multiple means of action and expression

This final pillar encourages us to think about flexibility in assessment, and how we might offer options when it comes to students demonstrating what they know.

In practice, this may look like:

- allowing students to complete tasks orally, in writing or through multimedia (for example, video, podcast)
- offering structured options like sentence starters, templates or guided prompts alongside open-ended tasks
- giving choice in assessment formats that measure the same learning outcomes (for example, group presentation/individual presentation, or phone-recorded oral voice over/in-person delivery/written presentation slides)
- using portfolios or ongoing project work to track progress instead of relying solely on one-off tests.

In focus: The CAST guidelines

The CAST (Center for Applied Special Technology) guidelines are a rich, research-backed resource with many layers of recommendations and suggestions for practice, consisting of nine core guidelines and 36 associated considerations.

They are well worth some exploration, and are freely available, here: https://udlguidelines.cast.org/

A rising tide lifts all ships...

Have you ever heard the idiom 'a rising tide lifts all ships'? As an autistic person, I don't *love* idioms – the more I try to untangle them, the less sense they make! But here, the idea is that when an improvement is made in one area – and it's often used in economic contexts – everyone will benefit. UDL is a perfect example of what this looks like in practice.

Often, teachers can feel concerned about 'time and effort required to support a proportionally small group of students', as researchers Newman and Conway found in a survey of Higher Education educators.[51] But designing for inclusion rarely benefits only a small subset of learners. Accessibility improvements often have wider-reaching effects – an idea known as the *curb-cut effect*, originally used to describe how ramps designed for wheelchair users also benefit parents with prams, delivery workers and many others.[52]

Reflecting on your practice

In this section we've thought about inclusion, rights and responsibilities and a pedagogical approach (UDL) that can help us to design and deliver more inclusive and accessible teaching. In Section Three, we'll turn our gaze from neurodiverse classrooms to neurodivergent learners and think more closely about some of the unique learning differences these learners bring.

Before we move on, here is another opportunity for you to reflect on how you might be able to integrate some of the ideas from this chapter into your teaching. If you turn to the Appendices at the end of this book, you'll find the second photocopiable tool on page 147: a *UDL Audit and Planner*. You can use this frame to help you reflect on how the three key principles of UDL – choice and flexibility in methods of engagement, representation, and action and expression – currently feature in your teaching practices.

You'll be prompted to consider how these principles currently show up in your materials, assessment tools and teaching methods as well as the learning environment itself. Across three columns, you'll have the space

---

51 Newman, I. and Conway, J. (2017) Busting the barriers to inclusive learning environments. *The Journal of Inclusive Practice in Further and Higher Education*, p.33.

52 Blackwell, A.G. (2017) The Curb-Cut Effect. *Stanford Social Innovation Review* [online]. Available at: https://ssir.org/articles/entry/the_curb_cut_effect (accessed January 2026).

to notice what's already working well and where barriers may exist, and to consider how you might adapt or expand your practice to make learning more flexible and accessible for all.

As with the tool in the previous chapter, this exercise is an invitation to audit your current practice and to identify where you can translate UDL theory into tangible teaching adjustments. It's not intended to be a way to criticise yourself if you realise there are areas where your teaching could be improved. We're all learning and adjusting, all the time.

TL:DR (too long: didn't read) summary

- *Universal Design* is a design philosophy originally developed in architecture to create environments, products and services that are usable by as many people as possible, regardless of age or ability. Examples include ramps, wide doors, lifts and low-floored buses.
- *Universal Design for Learning (UDL)* applies these principles to teaching and learning and plans to build in accessibility for all students from the outset, rather than relying on individual adjustments later.
- UDL assumes diversity from the start. It recognises that there is no such thing as an 'average student'. Because learners start from different places, and bring different abilities, needs, lived experience and learning preferences, the focus in UDL is on removing barriers rather than expecting students to adapt.
- UDL is structured around three key principles: the importance of providing *multiple methods of engagement* (with learning and the student experience); *multiple methods of representation* (of learning materials and information, i.e. in multiple formats); and *multiple methods of action and expression* (for example, flexible and varied approaches to assessment).
- Unlike traditional differentiation, which tailors lessons and adapts teaching for specific students after assessing needs, UDL builds flexibility into teaching from the start, making learning accessible to all.

- Inclusive design benefits everyone. This is sometimes called the *curb-cut effect* – a term that came from observing how ramps designed for wheelchair users also help parents with prams, delivery workers and many others.

Reflective questions

1. Thinking back to a time when you were a learner, did you benefit from any UDL features?
2. How might your learning experience have been different with more flexibility in engagement, representation or expression? What would you have most appreciated?
3. Think of a recent lesson where you naturally offered some degree of choice and flexibility in engagement, representation or expression. What worked well and what would you do differently next time?

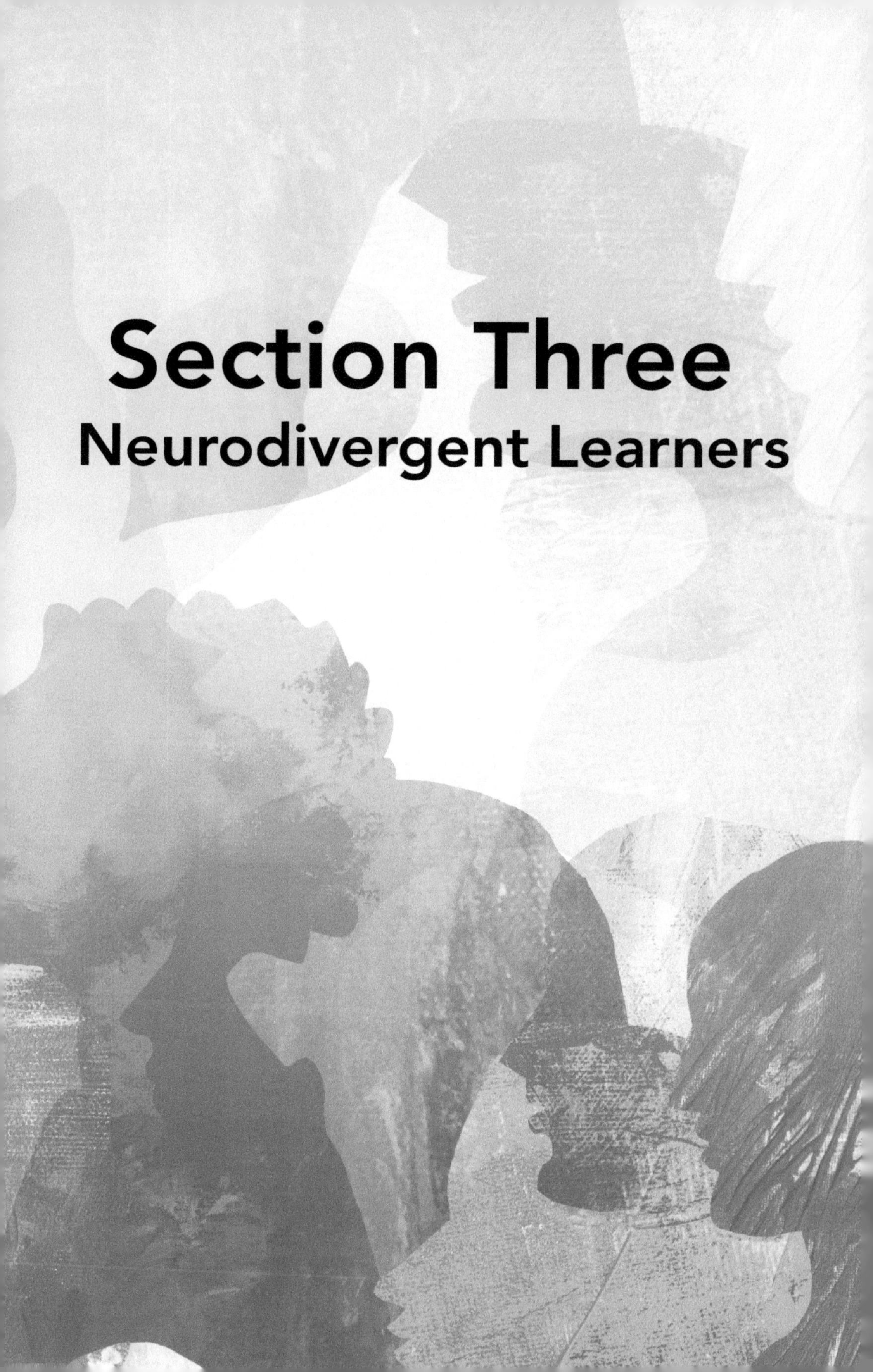

Section Three
Neurodivergent Learners

Chapter 5:
Communicating neurodivergent communication

By the end of this chapter you'll be able to:

- describe three key ideas from neurodiversity research (the *Double Empathy Problem*, *Monotropism* and *Gestalt Language Processing*) and explain their relevance to ELT
- recognise how *masking* behaviours may affect classroom interaction and participation
- apply insights from neurodivergent communication research to design classroom activities that support mutual understanding and engagement
- reflect on how differing communicative dispositions across neurotypes can shape learning, teaching and social connection.

The first half of this book has prioritised setting the scene and establishing a foundation of understanding difference. In Section One, we looked at the core concepts and history of neurodiversity and met a number of minority neurotypes in detail. In Section Two, we moved from ideas to implications and began to consider the neurodiverse classroom, exploring rights, responsibilities and UDL as a model for inclusion.

In Section Three, we're now moving our attention to neurodivergent learners. In Chapter 6 we'll consider global perspectives on neurodivergence and how different aspects of a learner's identity intersect to create unique learning needs and experiences. But first, in this chapter, we'll begin by looking in detail at some uniquely neurodivergent communicative, cognitive and behavioural characteristics that will no doubt have a bearing on language learning.

Different ways of 'languaging'

The neurodiversity perspective teaches us that there is a diverse range of human ways of being, thinking and doing. Much of human behaviour is measured and evaluated in terms of *norms* – although these norms vary between places and cultures. To exist outside of (locally determined) norms does not equate to being deficient in some way. One of the greatest things about humans is our diversity.

As language teachers, whether we realise it or not, we often guide learners to communicate in ways that fit within a narrow set of norms. Often, these are *native-speaker norms* – although these are gradually being deprioritised as English language communication is decolonialised and greater appreciation is given to different varieties of English (such as World Englishes, emergent varieties, and English as a Lingua Franca (ELF)).

Just as there are multiple varieties of English, that are equally valid, there are also multiple ways of *languaging*. Linguist Merrill Swain introduced the term 'languaging' to describe the 'process of making meaning and shaping knowledge and experience through language'.[53] The term invites us to understand language not as a static product or system to be mastered, but as an active process of mediating ideas, negotiating understanding and co-constructing meaning with others.

Because neurodivergent people process and experience things differently, they often *language* in different ways to neurotypical individuals, too. In fact, language-use atypicalities and social communication differences feature in the diagnostic criteria for many minority neurotypes (such as ADHD, autism, dyslexia, Tourette's. etc.).

53 Swain, M. (2006) Languaging, agency and collaboration in advanced second language learning. In: H. Byrnes (Ed.), *Advanced language learning: The contributions of Halliday and Vygotsky* (p.98). London, England: Continuum.

However, when communication breaks down between neurodivergent and neurotypical people, the blame is often placed on the neurodivergent communicator, reflecting a deficit view of communication in which any deviation from the majority norm is seen as a problem to be fixed. In the classroom, languaging differences can sometimes be misread as students not participating, as relying on limited recycled language, as off-topic contributions, or even as being disruptive.

But, as we know very well, communication is always a two-way process. It is a negotiation of meaning between people of sometimes very different positionalities. And while communicating through these differences can be hard, we also know that it *can* work, even when there are sparse shared language resources. For example, in encounters mediated by English as a Lingua Franca, speakers from sometimes vastly different cultural and first-language backgrounds regularly find common ground and co-construct both shared meaning and non-normative language forms that function as temporary, 'local' norms.[54] Diverse – and divergent – ways of languaging are important and legitimate expressions of *human* languaging. To be truly inclusive of neurodivergence, we need to work with how our learners work and, ultimately, support them in knowing how to navigate communication not only in a second language, but also across a neurotype divide (more on this in Chapter 7).

The following three neurodivergent-led theories of communicative, cognitive and language learning differences – the *Double Empathy Problem*, *Monotropism* and *Gestalt Language Processing* – will not necessarily be relevant for every minority neurotype, nor for every individual learner. However, by thinking about the different ways that neurodivergent learners engage with language learning and communication, we can broaden our understanding of human communication and develop teaching approaches that respond to diverse ways of languaging.

54 Jenkins, J., Cogo, A. and Dewey, M. (2011) Review of developments in research into English as a lingua franca. *Language Teaching*, 44(3): 281-315.

The Double Empathy Problem: Communicating across neurotypes

The best place to begin, in my opinion, when thinking about communication across neurotypes (or *cross-neurotype communication*), is a theory known as the Double Empathy Problem.

The concept was first proposed by autistic sociologist Damian Milton in 2012, and originally its focus was communication between autistic and non-autistic speakers.[55] Up until that point, autism theories had generally framed autistic people as impaired communicators. Autistic individuals were seen as lacking the ability to understand how others think and feel: while non-autistic people were seen as naturally socially skilled. When we think about language, and how much successful communication depends on 'reading between the lines' (for example, picking up what someone *means* as well as what they *say*), it's easy to see how the belief that autistic people can't imagine others' thoughts or intentions would lead to the idea that we're impaired communicators.

In focus: Autism and empathy – a stigmatising stereotype

The belief that autistic people struggle to empathise, or to understand the thoughts and feelings of others has long been debunked.

Autistic people experience empathy just as deeply as anyone else – sometimes more intensely – although it may be expressed differently.

This stereotype has caused real harm, shaping how autistic people are judged and misunderstood, but it's not supported by evidence.

Milton flipped this prevailing perspective and suggested that what's really going on is more a 'mismatch of salience'[56] between two 'differently disposed social actors'[57], with different ways of experiencing and

55 Milton, D.E., 2012. On the ontological status of autism: The 'double empathy problem'. *Disability & society*, 27(6), pp.883-887.

56 Milton, D.E. (2017) *A Mismatch of Salience*. Hove: Pavilion Publishing. This is a fantastic collection of Milton's early essays.

57 Milton, D.E. (2012) On the ontological status of autism: The 'double empathy problem'. *Disability & society*, 27 (6): 883-887.

interpreting the world. In other words, autistic and non-autistic people bring different assumptions and expectations to an interaction, which can make mutual understanding harder work. It's not that autistic people are inherently impaired communicators. It is a communication breakdown that goes *both ways*: it is a 'Double Empathy Problem'.

What the research shows us

Over the past decade or so, there has been a growing wave of research investigating and ultimately supporting the Double Empathy Problem, highlighting how communication difficulties really are a two-way issue in *cross-neurotype* exchanges.

Several studies, for example, have discovered how non-autistic people often struggle to interpret autistic facial expressions or emotional states of autistic individuals.[58] Non-verbal cues such as body language and facial expressions enrich our interpretations of what is being communicated in words. When our abilities to read these cues are reduced, our capacity to accurately interpret another's meaning is limited. When communication is taking place between autistic and non-autistic people, *both* parties may struggle to easily read these paralinguistic cues. However, because neurotypical communicative norms are dominant, it is usually the autistic speaker who is assumed to be the one misunderstanding or failing to communicate 'appropriately'.

Other research has shown that non-autistic people tend to form less favourable first impressions of autistic individuals; judgements that then shape how willing they are to interact with them. In one study, more than 200 non-autistic participants were asked to rate short video clips, audio recordings and still images of autistic and non-autistic people

---

58 There are many pieces of research published in this area now, but some good places to start include:

- Brewer, R., Biotti, F., Catmur, C., Press, C., Happé, F., Cook, R. & Bird, G. (2016) Can neurotypical individuals read autistic facial expressions? Atypical production of emotional facial expressions in autism spectrum disorders. *Autism Research*, 9(2): 262-271.
- Heasman, B. & Gillespie, A. (2018) Perspective-taking is two-sided: Misunderstandings between people with Asperger's syndrome and their family members. *Autism*, 22(6): 740-750.
- Sheppard, E., Pillai, D., Wong, G.T.L., Ropar, D. & Mitchell, P. (2016) How easy is it to read the minds of people with autism spectrum disorder? *Journal of Autism and Developmental Disorders*, 46(4): 1247-1254.

auditioning for a mock reality show.[59] They rated each person for qualities such as attractiveness, likeability, trustworthiness, and how willing they would be to start a conversation or live near them. Across all formats, the autistic participants were rated significantly more negatively than the non-autistic participants. However, when the same researchers presented participants with *written transcripts* of the audition videos – showing only the words that had been spoken, with no image or sound – the difference disappeared. The autistic and non-autistic participants were rated equally when only their words were visible. These findings highlight that the issue wasn't *what* was said, but *how* the autistic speakers were perceived. Again, this likely has something to do with subtle differences in paralinguistic communication – tone, pitch, speech rhythm, facial expressions, body language – but here it points less to a barrier to understanding and more to an intolerance of difference.

In focus: 'Masking' – self-protection in a judgemental

Because autistic people often encounter repeated negative judgements and misunderstandings in social interactions, many adopt a strategy known as 'masking' or 'camouflaging' to manage how they are perceived.

Masking can involve consciously or unconsciously adapting their behaviour to fit in; observing and mimicking the speech and behaviours of peers, following rehearsed social scripts, mirroring gestures or suppressing behaviours that might be judged as 'different'.

Masking is not simply 'trying to appear neurotypical'. It is a form of self-protection in a world that penalises difference. Over time, masking can become a complex, layered practice of emotional, social and physical regulation, helping autistic people navigate environments that might otherwise be hostile or unsafe. However, *this protective strategy carries a high cost.* Research links frequent masking to exhaustion, burnout, mental health challenges and, in some cases, suicidal ideation.

59 Sasson, N.J., Faso, D.J., Nugent, J., Lovell, S., Kennedy, D.P. & Grossman, R.B. (2017) Neurotypical peers are less willing to interact with those with autism based on thin slice judgments. *Scientific Reports*, 7(1): 40700.

While masking is most often associated with autistic people – and autistic women and girls in particular – it is a strategy that many neurodivergent people may engage with at times.

In the ELT classroom

Masking can also affect classroom participation. Language classrooms often reward conformity to native-like speech norms, but many native-like norms of any given language are also *neurotypical* norms. As such, masking can sometimes become part of language performance, requiring learners to suppress natural communication patterns. Potential consequences of this include an increased cognitive load, heightened anxiety and a loss of the person's authentic voice. Students who are actively managing how they are perceived may be also appear quieter or be less likely to volunteer answers.

Recommended reading:

Pearson, A. & Rose, K. (2023) *Autistic masking: Understanding identity management and the role of stigma*. Pavilion Publishing

Finally, there's also now plenty of evidence that communication between autistic interlocutors can be fluent and rewarding. In one study, autistic participants reported that talking to other autistic people felt easier: 'they totally get it'.[60] In another, researchers observed that, in groups made up entirely of autistic adults, conversation flowed naturally, even when it didn't follow typical turn-taking patterns. Topic shifts, tangents and pauses were tolerated without awkwardness, and shared humour often developed quickly.[61] All together, these studies show that communication differences between autistic and non-autistic people are largely relational, not individual.

Beyond autism

Although the Double Empathy Problem began as a theory of communication between autistic and non-autistic people, its core message can, I believe, be applied to *all* cross-neurotype interaction.

60 Crompton, C.J., Fletcher-Watson, S. & Ropar, D. (2019a) 'I never realised everybody felt as happy as I do when I am around autistic people': a thematic analysis of autistic adults' relationships with autistic and neurotypical friends and family. *Autism*, 24(6): 1443.

61 Heasman, B. & Gillespie, A., (2019) Neurodivergent intersubjectivity: Distinctive features of how autistic people create shared understanding. *Autism*, 23(4): 910-921.

The Double Empathy Problem looks at interactions between people from different experiential worlds – with cognitive, attentional and sensory profiles that can feel alien to one another. This could just as easily describe communication between people with ADHD and people without, between people with and without acquired brain injuries, or between someone with Tourette's and someone with PTSD. What looks like disinterest to one person might simply be focus or sensory regulation to another. What feels like warmth to one speaker might read as overfamiliarity to someone else. The combinations are endless – what matters is that when people with differences in attention, processing, behaviour or social expectations try to connect, it can often take more work to find common ground.[62]

The Double Empathy Problem in the ELT classroom

As language teachers who often mediate multilingual and multicultural social spaces, we are already skilled at navigating difference. Neurodivergent ways of languaging and learning are just further dimensions of difference for us to accommodate and make space for.

In practical terms, some things to consider include:

- **Remembering that the Double Empathy Problem can affect teacher-student communication:** If learners don't appear to be understanding, it may not necessarily be a second-language issue.
- **Asking students why:** Try to avoid making assumptions about behaviour (based on neurotypical norms) before inviting students to share their perspective, and be aware of implicit biases.
- **Allowing flexible language use:** Make space for variation, especially for functional or social language. Different ways of communicating can still be meaningful, even if they don't follow the usual 'rules'.
- **Celebrating different strategies:** Highlight creative or alternative ways students solve language tasks. It shows that multiple approaches are valid.

62 I've written a whole other book – *Understanding Others in a Neurodiverse World* – that looks in much more detail at how we navigate differences in salience and how to operationalise this 'extra work' from a cognitive linguistics perspective, if that's your thing...

- **Modelling and practising repair strategies:** Show and encourage ways to handle misunderstandings, so students can navigate miscommunication confidently.

Monotropism: Deep focus and different patterns of attention

Many neurodivergent people – in particular autistic individuals and those with ADHD and AuDHD – tend to have atypical attention allocation, which may ultimately shape how they learn and engage in classroom activities. The theory of *monotropism*, first proposed by autistic researchers Dinah Murray, Mike Lesser and Wenn Lawson in 2005, helps us to understand these differences.[63]

Attention is a precious commodity in the language classroom, shaping everything from activity design to classroom management. Those familiar with the study of (second) language acquisition will also recognise 'attention' as an integral ingredient in the process of turning language input into intake (i.e. acquired language). Schmidt's influential 'Noticing Hypothesis', for example, highlights how second language learning is largely driven by what learners pay attention to.[64] While it's not been universally agreed that conscious noticing of an input is necessary for new language acquisition, there's no doubt that attention shapes what's acquired and underpins learning.

The theory of monotropism takes as its starting point the (fairly uncontested) idea that attention is a limited cognitive resource. We cannot pay attention to all things at all times, so our minds are constantly prioritising what to focus on and what to filter out. For most people, attention is distributed across many different areas and stimuli at once in a broader but slightly more diluted way – a pattern referred to as *polytropic* attention. For many autistic, ADHD or AuDHD individuals, attention is often more narrowly and intensely focused in specific directions – a pattern referred to as *monotropic* attention.

63 Murray, D., Lesser, M. and Lawson, W., 2005. Attention, monotropism and the diagnostic criteria for autism. *Autism*, 9(2), pp.139-156

64 Schmidt, R. (1990) The role of consciousness in second language learning. *Applied Linguistics*, 11: 129-158

A useful way to think about the difference between these two patterns is to imagine different kinds of light in a dark room. A neurotypical (polytropic) mind has a wide, soft lamp that lights up a large portion of the room, allowing lots of things to be seen at once. A monotropic mind, by contrast, shines a bright torch intensely in one small area. It illuminates incredible detail within that focused spot but only captures what falls inside the beam. This intense focus can create profound expertise over the long term and deep engagement in the short term, but it also means that things outside the light tunnel (for example, verbal instructions, physical sensations) might be overlooked in the moment.

When attention is highly absorbed in this way, it can often feel deeply rewarding, and similar to the experience of 'being in the flow' (where you lose track of time and everything seems to happen with great ease and joy). Sudden externally imposed shifts (such new task demands or a change in the sensory environment) can feel abrupt or even distressing. For some, unexpected interruptions to an intense attentional tunnel can rupture a sense of safety or self-regulation. In the classroom, what might look like resistance to change or difficulty transitioning may, in fact, reflect the discomfort of being forcibly pulled out of deep focus and flow.

Monotropism in the ELT classroom

Monotropism helps explain why some neurodivergent learners become fully absorbed in a topic – sometimes to the exclusion of all else – and why interruptions or sudden changes can feel overwhelming. It also offers insights into behaviours often associated with autism and ADHD: like repetitive actions, strong interests and variable sensory experiences (where some sensory information falls intensely within the attention tunnel, and some barely registers).

In terms of teaching and learning, one recent study investigating monotropism and its application in the classroom found that participants with high monotropic tendencies 'preferred to learn autodidactically and had a preference to focus on tasks for longer periods of time as opposed to shorter tasks'.[65] They also reported leaning into their monotropic interests as a means of self-regulating, staying calm and enhancing their learning.

65 Atkinson, A. (2026) An Interest-Based Exploration of Monotropism and Its Use in the Classroom. In: *Neurodivergent Education and Lifelong Learning* (pp. 129-146). IGI Global Scientific Publishing.

With all this in mind, some practical considerations include:

- **Allowing flow time:** When a student is 'in the zone', try to give them uninterrupted time to explore a task. Flow is where learning feels effortless and rewarding and it is a great opportunity to strengthen skills.
- **Supporting attention shifts:** Help students manage transitions between tasks or topics, using clear cues, timely warnings and gentle scaffolding.
- **Valuing depth over breadth:** Provide opportunities for and celebrate detailed exploration, not just speed or coverage of multiple tasks.
- **Facilitating the integrating of a monotropic learner's intense interests:** 'Special interests', as they're sometimes called), should be included in the curriculum of teaching or project work.
- **Considering if monotropic learners might prefer to work by themselves or need additional time on tasks:** For certain tasks or activities, be flexible as to whether tasks can be completed alone or in groups and what the time limit is for those tasks.
- **Providing support or extra time when multitasking is necessary:** Monotopic learners may find tasks that demand multitasking, rapid shifts in focus, or simultaneous processing of multiple streams of information more challenging.

Gestalt Language Processing: Learning (and speaking) in chunks

The Double Empathy Problem shows us that understanding is a two-way process that can be complicated in communication across neurotypes, where speakers have markedly different cognitive and embodied experiences. Monotropism highlights how attention allocation can vary significantly between individuals, shaping how we learn and engage with interests and the world around us. Both these neurodivergent-led theories are now fairly well accepted and supported by research and scholarly literature.

There is one further theory that has been adopted in recent years by some of the neurodivergent community that describes differences in language acquisition that is worth mentioning here: *Gestalt Language Processing*. There is, currently, limited empirical evidence to support the theory, but many individuals feel it accurately describes their experiences and it is a concept that has gained popularity, including among some Speech and Language Therapists.[66]

Echolalia

Echolalia is a term used to refer to the repetition of words or phrases heard previously, either immediately after they are heard (*immediate echolalia*) or after a delay of hours, days, or even years (*delayed echolalia*). It is a typical stage in early first-language acquisition for all children, but for many autistic people and some others, echolalia continues as a natural part of communication throughout life (or reappears later in life, as is the case in dementia or aphasia, for example). Echolalic utterances may be as brief as a single word (for example, 'Chrysanthemum!'[67] – *an autumn-flowering perennial flowering plant*) or as long as a song, or a whole film script.

Historically, echolalia was considered to be an uncommunicative or meaningless symptom of language impairment. However, as understandings of autism and neurodivergence have shifted away from the medical model towards a more neurodiversity-affirming, social model, echolalia's communicative purposes are being increasingly recognised. In addition to autistic and neurodivergent testimony that echolalia is meaningful, a growing number of academic studies of naturally occurring autistic communication have shown that echoed speech can serve a range of functions: to redirect a conversation, to protest, to self-soothe, or to share experience.[68] Other studies have similarly demonstrated that echolalia can be generative, enabling speakers to adapt familiar language to express novel meanings. For example, one child (Bud) who loved the TV show the *Teletubbies* began by echoing the line 'One day in Teletubbyland, all of the Teletubbies were very busy when suddenly

66 Hutchins, T.L., Knox, S.E. & Fletcher, E.C. (2024) Natural language acquisition and gestalt language processing: A critical analysis of their application to autism and speech language therapy. *Autism & Developmental Language Impairments*, 9, p.23969415241249944.

67 'Chrysanthemum' is one of the single-word echolalic utterances that early autism scientist, Leo Kanner, documented his child patient repeating in 1943 that shaped the autism diagnostic profile. In: Kanner, L. (1943) Autistic disturbances of affective contact. *Nervous Child*, 2(3): 217-250.

68 For example, see Sterponi, L. & de Kirby, K. (2016) A multidimensional reappraisal of language in autism: Insights from a discourse analytic study. *Journal of Autism and Developmental Disorders*, 46(2): 394-405.

a big rain cloud appeared', but later reworked it into 'One day in Bud's house, Mama and Bud were very busy when suddenly Daddy appeared' to express the excitement of his father coming home.[69]

Gestalts

The word 'gestalt' (from the German for 'form' or 'shape') refers to perceiving something as an integrated whole rather than as separate parts. The idea of *Gestalt Language Processing* was first discussed in the early 1980s as a non-pathologising way of understanding patterns of language use seen particularly among autistic speakers. All children acquire language through a combination of *analytic* and *gestalt* processes – learning some words and grammatical structures unit by unit, while also absorbing and using larger chunks or familiar phrases as wholes. The central idea of Gestalt Language Processing is that, for some individuals, particularly autistic or otherwise neurodivergent people, this gestalt mode of processing is dominant and remains so throughout development.

In this account, gestalt processing describes learning and using multi-word 'chunks' as whole semantic units before understanding their granular lexical or grammatical structure. Over time, speakers may begin to modify these units, gradually segmenting and recombining them into new, flexible forms of expression. Gestalts often have idiosyncratic, emotional meanings tied to specific contexts, enriched by specific prosodies, the depth of which may not be immediately obvious to a listener.[70]

The essential premise of Gestalt Language Processing is that some autistic and neurodivergent people tend towards a top-down rather than a bottom-up means of language acquisition. While there remains some debate within academic circles about the theory's current ability to support its claims, many autistic and neurodivergent people identify with this description of their engagement with language, and for that reason alone it is worth thinking about seriously.

---

69 Gernsbacher, M.A., Morson, E.M. & Grace, E.J. (2016) Language and speech in autism. *Annual Review of Linguistics*, 2: 413-425.

70 Have you seen the film 'Ace Ventura Pet Detective'? If you have, try to say (out loud or inside to yourself) his catchphrase *'Alrighty then'*. Isn't it imbued with deliciously silly feeling and an impossibly catchy intonation? (If you haven't seen the film, a quick YouTube search of the phrase will satisfy your curiosity).

Gestalt Language Processing' in the ELT classroom

Gestalt Language Processing appears to have a lot in common with the fundamentals of a second-language learning theory that many teachers may already be familiar with: the *lexical approach*.[71] The lexical approach is a language teaching methodology that emphasises lexical chunks (for example, collocations, fixed phrases, idioms and other commonly co-occurring word combinations) as the primary building blocks of language, rather than focusing solely on individual words or grammar rules. The lexical approach is based on the principle that language is primarily *grammaticalised lexis, not lexicalised grammar*: highlighting the importance of learning words in context rather than in isolation.

This perspective on language – as a collection of meaningful chunks – offers a practical way of thinking about how learners with gestalt processing preferences might engage with language in the classroom.

Practical considerations include:

- **Incorporating the lexical approach into activities or the curriculum:** Encourage learners to identify and record lexical chunks and fixed phrases in texts they read or listen to new language.
- **Providing repeated exposure to multi-word phrases:** Use many different contexts to support internalisation and recall.
- **Explore chunk recycling:** Invite learners to reuse familiar phrases or scripts from earlier lessons or favourite media, and encourage them to explore ways in which they might be adapted or extended for new communicative contexts.

In summary

Across these three neurodiversity-affirming theories, we've seen how communication differences traditionally interpreted as language 'impairment' in neurodivergence, might instead be reframed as simply *different ways of languaging*. Social communication difficulties and breakdowns in understanding between neurotypes can be viewed, more helpfully, as differences in expectations and ways of processing between two 'differently disposed social actors' – an issue that can also shape teacher-student interactions. Apparent difficulties with concentration and

71 Lewis, M. (1993) *The Lexical Approach* (Vol. 1, p. 993). Hove: Language Teaching Publications.

engagement with learning might be better thought about in terms of drastically divergent attentional styles, that require structure and support. Challenges with learning a second language declaratively, from the bottom up, might be mitigated by providing more opportunities to recycle and rework larger lexical chunks and to focus more on functional language.

In this chapter, we've explored how communication and behaviour can vary across neurotypes, how neurodivergent ways of languaging may not always match up with neurotypical norms but how, importantly, *difference* does not mean *deficit*. However, consciously knowing and agreeing with this perspective doesn't necessarily mean our actions always align. Unconscious (or *implicit*) biases are social stereotypes about certain groups of people that form outside our conscious awareness. We all carry them – it's part of how human brains make sense of the world – but left unexamined they can influence how we perceive and respond to others we experience as different to ourselves.

Despite the growth of the neurodiversity paradigm, stigma and misinformation around neurodivergence remain prevalent in media and public discourse. It's very easy to internalise these negative assumptions and popular prejudices about neurodivergent people and let them shape our interactions, but by becoming aware of our biases we can take steps toward changing them. On page 148 you'll find a photocopiable reflective tool designed to help teachers notice, name, and critically examine implicit neurodivergent biases. Across three supported steps, readers are guided through identifying their unfiltered first impressions, any potential implicit judgements about atypical learner behaviours alongside a reflection on how these judgements map onto minority neurotypes and, finally, a perspective-taking activity focussed on classroom experience.

In the next chapter, we'll continue to think about human variety and explore how neurodivergence intersects with other aspects of our learners' identities...

TL:DR (too long: didn't read) summary

- Neurodivergent people often communicate in atypical ways. In the past, these were sometimes described as language 'impairments'. The neurodiversity perspective reframes these as simply *differences.*
- In the same way that there are many legitimate varieties of English around the world, there are also many valid ways of *languaging* (i.e. communicating, making meaning and mediating thought, through language). Neurodivergent people may *language* differently to neurotypical people.
- The *Double Empathy Problem* is a theory that first addressed the communication breakdowns between autistic and neurotypical people – but it can be relevant for many cross-neurotype interactions. It is now backed by a large body of research demonstrating that communication breakdowns between autistic and non-autistic people are mutual, not one-sided.
- According to the Double Empathy Problem, misunderstandings arise from differing expectations, communication styles and lived experience on both sides – not from any inherent inability on the autistic person's part (as was historically thought).
- Many neurodivergent people hide or suppress their natural behaviours (as well as natural communication patterns) and aspects of their personality to avoid stigma – a process known as *masking.* Masking is a valid response to a world that can be hostile to those who appear different, but it comes at a cost to the individual's mental and physical health in the long term.
- Autistic people and those with ADHD have divergent attention patterns to most neurotypical people – a theory known as *monotropism.* Narrow but intense attention tunnels can support deep learning and engagement (in tasks of interest), but can make sudden shifts or multitasking challenging.
- Some neurodivergent people are thought to primarily acquire and use language in chunks (gestalts) rather than discrete words or grammar rules – a theory known as *Gestalt Language Processing* that doesn't yet have conclusive evidence. The lexical approach (a common ELT methodology) can support learners who appear to learn this way.

Reflective questions

1. Are there any features of your current teaching practice or classroom culture that might unintentionally reward masking? What small steps could you take to reduce that pressure for neurodivergent learners?
2. Is your view of 'appropriate' communication influenced by neurotypical norms? If so, which of these can be loosened a little, and in what contexts?
3. How could you accommodate learners with monotropic attentional styles within your current lesson planning?
4. What opportunities exist in your classroom to notice, celebrate and build on students' natural communication preferences or interests?

Chapter 6: Intersectionality and decolonial perspectives

By the end of this chapter you'll be able to:

- give examples of how different neurodivergences can co-occur
- relate an understanding of the body-brain connection in neurodivergence to certain learner behaviours and experiences
- describe the concept of 'intersectionality'
- recognise how different dimensions of a learner's identity may either mask their neurodivergence or elicit greater stigma
- better predict cultural differences in attitudes towards neurodivergence.

In the previous chapter, we narrowed the focused from the wider lens of neurodiverse classrooms, to take a closer look at individual neurodivergent learners and at common communicative differences they may have. We considered how neurotypical norms shape communication more generally, as well as the ways in which we perceive and interact with students, often without conscious awareness. Building on that, this chapter explores the broader context in which these learners exist. We'll see how neurodivergent learners rarely have a single form of neurodivergence and how intersecting aspects of a learner's identity, along with differing global social and cultural factors, influence how they are seen and understood.

The multiplicity of neurodivergence

As we begin to focus more closely on individual learners and their neurodivergent needs, it's important to note that neurodivergence rarely occurs in neat, isolated categories. Many learners will have multiple co-occurring neurodivergences or a blend of traits that cut across diagnostic boundaries. Not all of these will be formally diagnosed. Some learners will be aware of their neurodivergent traits or self-identify as neurodivergent but lack formal diagnoses (for any number of very valid reasons, such as fear of stigma or lack of access to timely diagnostic services). Others may exhibit neurodivergent traits but either not wish to take on the neurodivergent or diagnostic label, or have not had the opportunity to consider it. Finally, some learners (like me) may have a primary neurodivergence diagnosed (in my case, autism) with other neurodivergent traits (in my case, dyscalculic traits) that have never been assessed.

If this sounds like I am about to suggest you start trying to guess your learners' neurodivergences, worry not! It isn't your role as a teacher to play sleuth. In fact, trying to do so can risk reinforcing stereotypes or creating unnecessary pressures for both you and your learner (particularly if they don't yet identify as neurodivergent). Within a Universal Design for Learning approach, the emphasis on creating flexible, accessible learning experiences up-front that support all learners means that disclosure of diagnoses is rarely necessary (while learners whose more individual needs are not pre-emptively met can still request reasonable adjustments). However, having a good foundational understanding of how neurodivergences commonly co-occur can help you anticipate potential challenges and tailor your teaching more effectively.

The following figures illustrate some of the more common overlaps in neurodivergence we currently know about, highlighting where connections often occur. While not exhaustive, they provide a useful reference for understanding the multiplicity of traits you may encounter in your classroom.

Crossovers and connections:

- Around 50-70% of autistic people also have ADHD ('AuDHD').[72]
- Up to 85% of people with a tic condition have an additional neurodivergence.[73]
- Around 80% of autistic people have dyspraxia-like traits.[74]
- Around 50% of people with dyspraxia have ADHD.[75]
- Neurodivergent people are twice as likely to be hypermobile.[76]
- Around 21% of autistic people have a chronic pain condition (such as ME or fibromyalgia).[77]

Brain-body connection

You may have noticed that the final two bullet points above touch on physical health. It is only in very recent years that we are beginning to understand the *brain-body connection* in neurodivergence. For some time, we've recognised the high co-occurrence rate of mental health conditions such as anxiety, depression and disordered eating among neurodivergent individuals. What we now know is that this connection extends beyond mental health. Chronic pain conditions, gastrointestinal disorders and fatigue, along with dermatological,

72 Hours, C., Recasens, C. & Baleyte, J.M. (2022) ASD and ADHD comorbidity: What are we talking about? *Frontiers in Psychiatry*, 13, p.837424.

73 Martino, D., Ganos, C. & Pringsheim, T.M. (2017) Tourette syndrome and chronic tic disorders: the clinical spectrum beyond tics. *International Review of Neurobiology*, 134, pp.1461-1490.

74 Gowen, E. & Hamilton, A. (2013) Motor abilities in autism: a review using a computational context. *Journal of autism and developmental disorders*, 43(2), pp.323-344.

75 Goulardins, J.B., Rigoli, D., Licari, M., Piek, J.P., Hasue, R.H., Oosterlaan, J. & Oliveira, J.A. (2015) Attention deficit hyperactivity disorder and developmental coordination disorder: Two separate disorders or do they share a common etiology. *Behavioural Brain Research*, 292, pp.484-492.

76 Csecs, J.L., Iodice, V., Rae, C.L., Brooke, A., Simmons, R., Quadt, L., Savage, G.K., Dowell, N.G., Prowse, F., Themelis, K. & Mathias, C.J. (2022) Joint hypermobility links neurodivergence to dysautonomia and pain. *Frontiers in Psychiatry*, 12, p.786916.

77 Grant, S., Norton, S., Weiland, R.F., Scheeren, A.M., Begeer, S. & Hoekstra, R.A. (2022) Autism and chronic ill health: an observational study of symptoms and diagnoses of central sensitivity syndromes in autistic adults. *Molecular Autism*, 13(1), p.7.

immunological and respiratory disorders often co-exist alongside neurodivergence as a cluster of whole-body traits, now thought to be mediated by differences in connective tissue.[78]

In the classroom

In practical terms, these whole-body differences can show up in subtle but important ways in the classroom. Some learners may find standard classroom furniture (for example, hard chairs, low desks) uncomfortable or even painful, and may benefit from softer or more ergonomic alternatives. Where options in seating type isn't possible or practical, allowing learners to stand or adjust their posture throughout the lesson – including to unconventional sitting positions – can provide a significant difference. Similarly, some learners may need to stand, stretch, shift position, or move around intermittently to regulate pain, dizziness or energy levels. Allowing movement without framing it as disruptive behaviour can support engagement and help learners feel more comfortable.

Some learners may require more frequent bathroom breaks but not wish to draw attention to themselves by having to ask for permission to leave. Flexible, low-pressure routines can help reduce anxiety around this. For learners with autonomic nervous system dysregulation, activities that raise stress levels (such as high-pressure presentation tasks, sudden transitions, competitive games or timed tests) may trigger responses such as increased heart rate, dizziness or fatigue. Providing alternatives or advance warning can help learners pace themselves. For those with chronic pain or fatigue conditions, maintaining energy and concentration levels across a course may be harder. Offering choice in task intensity and pacing helps learners engage when they can, without being penalised when they can't.

---

78 These connections are still very recent discoveries and not yet widely reported or understood. In addition to the Csecs et al. (2022) citation above (note 74), you can find more information at:

- The Sussex Partnership NHS Foundation Trust – Neurodivergent Brain-Body Clinic (www.sussexpartnership.nhs.uk/our-research/mental-health-dementia-research/research-clinics/neurodivergent-brain-body-clinic)
- SEDSConnective (www.sedsconnective.org)
- All Brains Belong (www.allbrainsbelong.org/all-the-things)

Because many learners may not disclose these underlying physical needs (and indeed, are under no obligation to), building flexibility into seating, movement, pacing and task formats helps ensure learners can participate without having to explain or justify what their bodies require.

Intersectionality and neurodivergence

'When we are not intersectional, we are not relevant.'

– Atif Choudhury, CEO of Diversity and Ability[79]

The term *intersectionality*, like 'neurodiversity', is one that has rocketed into the common vernacular in recent years and so may be something you're already familiar with. Originally coined by Kimberlé Crenshaw – a Black, American civil rights advocate and professor of critical race theory – and founded in the work of the Black feminist movement, the term offers a way of thinking about the influences of power and privilege on an individual.[80]

It takes a holistic view of a person's identity and recognises that one person has many different aspects that combine to make them who they are. Besides the many different roles we have in life (like teacher, student, parent, sibling, friend, boss, worker, carer, etc.) there are some fundamental parts of who we are that society often stereotypes and treats differently or values in a certain way. The intersectional perspective recognises that different elements of our identities (such as gender, race, class, sexuality, religion, etc.) elicit various degrees of privilege and discrimination – or, more often than not, a complex mixture of both.

Sylvia Duckworth, an author and educator from Canada, has created a really helpful infographic that illustrates how a person can have power and privilege from some aspects of their identity, and face discrimination or marginalisation on account of other aspects of their identity.

79 This quote is taken from Atif Choudhury's Foreword in Brissett-Bailey, M. (Ed.) (2023) *Black, Brilliant and Dyslexic: Neurodivergent heroes tell their stories.* Jessica Kingsley Publishers.

80 Crenshaw, K. (1989) Demarginalizing the intersection of race and sex: a black feminist critique of antidiscrimination doctrine, feminist theory and antiracist politics. *University of Chicago Legal Forum*: 1(8): 139-167.

Figure 6.1: A pastel-coloured infographic by Sylvia Duckworth demonstrating the intersections of power and marginalisation based on different aspects of an individual's identity. Full image description at the end of the chapter.

In the *Wheel of Power/Privilege*, the dimensions of an individual's identity that elicit the most power are those located closest to the centre of the circle. As English language teachers, it's an interesting temporary diversion to reflect on the fact that being a speaker of English has been placed at the centre: with non-English monolingual speakers placed at the far edge of marginalisation. I suspect this is more about the context in which the design was created – Canada, in the Global North. However, it may be worth considering which languages sit closest to the centre of the wheel in your teaching contexts, and which may sit at the centre of a global wheel of power/privilege in 20- or 30-years' time.

Some of the characteristics at the centre of the wheel may be familiar from another parallel concept we encountered in Chapter 4: the idea of the *mythical norm*. Audre Lorde's suggestion was that we are all essentially measured up against a narrow and exclusionary (and essentially impossible) standard – a mythical norm – that regulates who is seen to belong in society or who deserves to hold power.

The mythical norm (as represented by those characteristics in the centre of the wheel) is important to hold in mind when we are thinking about neurodivergence: as much of our early and foundational understanding and beliefs about different minority neurotypes has been shaped by it. The early clinicians who developed the diagnostic criteria, the first patients they saw, the early scientists and the participants that have generally been included in research have all been individuals closest to the mythical norm (for example, affluent, white and male).[81] The result is that a large portion of what we know about many minority neurotypes is biased and misses many intersecting perspectives and experiences – in particular those of women and girls, Black, Brown and racially minoritised individuals in the Global North, Global South citizens, and older neurodivergent people. Below, we'll look at some of intersectional differences we *do* know about...

Sex, gender and sexuality

Because early research and diagnoses focused on a narrow group of people, we still have an incomplete picture of how sex, gender and sexuality relate to neurodivergence. Even so, some consistent patterns have emerged.

A 'missed generation' of women and girls

Boys are currently diagnosed with autism or ADHD around three to four times more often than girls,[82] and they are typically referred for

81 I look at this in a lot more detail in Williams, G. (2024) *Understanding Others in a Neurodiverse World: A radical perspective on communication and shared meaning*. Hove: Pavilion Publishing.

82 For autism rates and diagnostic biases, see, for example, Loomes, R., Hull, L. & Mandy, W.P.L. (2017) What is the male-to-female ratio in autism spectrum disorder? A systematic review and meta-analysis. *Journal of the American Academy of Child & Adolescent Psychiatry*, 56(6), pp.466-474.

For ADHD rates, see, for example, Young, S., Adamo, N., Ásgeirsdóttir, B.B., Branney, P., Beckett, M., Colley, W., Cubbin, S., Deeley, Q., Farrag, E., Gudjonsson, G. & Hill, P. (2020) Females with ADHD: An expert consensus statement taking a lifespan approach providing guidance for the identification and treatment of attention-deficit/hyp eractivity disorder in girls and women. *BMC Psychiatry*, 20(1), p.404.

assessment at a younger age.[83] Yet studies consistently show that boys and men are more likely to be referred for diagnostic and support services even when girls and women present with very similar needs or behaviours. This shows us that the higher rates of diagnoses reflects diagnostic bias, not true prevalence.

The result is what many have described as a 'missed generation' of women and people assigned female at birth (AFAB) who have grown up without recognition or support for their neurodivergence. Many only seek or receive a diagnosis in adulthood, after years of internalising the belief that their differences were personal shortcomings: a pattern that can be both exhausting and profoundly isolating, often leading to burnout or mental health issues later in life.

Sexuality and gender diversity

There seems to be a substantial overlap between neurodivergent and LGBTQIA+ communities. Autistic people, in particular, are significantly more likely than non-autistic people to identify as lesbian, gay, bisexual, queer, asexual or otherwise non-heterosexual.[84] Gender diversity is also more common in neurodivergent groups – again, with research so far primarily focusing on autistic individuals.[85] One study often cited in this area compared autistic and non-autistic people's experiences of their gender identity.[86] Autistic participants showed a broader range of gender identities and more gender-dysphoric traits than their non-autistic peers, with the biggest differences among autistic people who had been assigned female at birth.

Sexism, homophobia and transphobia are issues that many English language teachers may have had to carefully navigate at some time or another. English language classrooms are often multicultural, representing a variety of cultural backgrounds and religious beliefs that do not always

83 Lai, M.C., Amestoy, A., Bishop, S., Brown, H.M., Onaiwu, M.G., Halladay, A., Harrop, C., Hotez, E., Huerta, M., Kelly, A. & Miller, D (2023) Improving autism identification and support for individuals assigned female at birth: clinical suggestions and research priorities. *The Lancet Child & Adolescent Health*, 7(12), pp.897-908.

84 Weir, E., Allison, C. & Baron-Cohen, S. (2021) The sexual health, orientation, and activity of autistic adolescents and adults. *Autism Research*, 14(11), pp.2342-2354.

85 Davidson, J. & Tamas, S. (2016) Autism and the ghost of gender. *Emotion, Space and Society*, 19: 59-65.

86 George, R. & Stokes, M.A. (2018) Gender identity and sexual orientation in autism spectrum disorder. *Autism*, 22(8), pp.970-982.

see eye-to-eye. Recognising how sex, gender and sexuality intersect with neurodivergence can help us better understand our learners' experiences and build classrooms where every student is met with dignity and safety.

Race and ethnicity

Black, Brown, Asian and racially minoritised people have historically been underrepresented in both diagnostic statistics and neurodiversity research. Although this picture is beginning to shift, significant disparities remain. As a result, many neurodivergent people of colour grow up without recognition or support, even when their behaviours or learning profiles mirror those of white peers who receive diagnoses earlier. Again, as with the diagnostic rate discrepancies between sexes, the issue is not prevalence but inequity in visibility and access.

In some minority ethnic or religious communities, stigma around neurodivergence or limited access to culturally relevant and translated information can discourage families from seeking assessment. Where structural racism affects access to healthcare and education, referral pathways may be slower or more circuitous. The result is, again, a pattern of underdiagnosis and lack of support.

The inequities experienced by Black neurodivergent people and those from minoritised ethnicities also extend to safety. Black autistic people, for example, are disproportionately exposed to harm, particularly during encounters with law enforcement, where their atypical communication or movement is often misread as defiance or aggression. There are numerous documented cases of Black autistic boys and men being criminalised or violently restrained when their behaviours are misread as threatening.[87] In countries such as the USA, these encounters have often, tragically, resulted in fatalities. This dangerous combination of racism and ableism that racially minoritised and neurodivergent individuals face is sometimes described as a 'double minority status'.

For individuals with these intersecting identities, social encounters are often complicated by a complex web of stigma and misunderstanding. For example, in a recent study by doctoral researcher Tiffany Nelson, Black autistic girls aged 16–18 described navigating both racism and

---

87 Hutson, T.M., Hassrick, E.M., Fernandes, S., Walton, J., Bouvier-Weinberg, K., Radcliffe, A. & Allen-Handy, A. (2022) 'I'm just different–that's all–I'm so sorry...': Black men, ASD and the urgent need for DisCrit Theory in police encounters. *Policing: An International Journal*, 45(3): 524-537.

microaggressions at school that intertwined with ableist assumptions about autism.[88] This is perhaps unsurprising when we consider how Black girls and boys are often stereotyped as more aggressive or disruptive than their white peers. When such racialised expectations intersect with autistic traits (for example, speaking frankly, challenging perceived injustice, having expressive meltdowns, or simply having a louder, less regulated voice) the result can be a heightened risk of misinterpretation and punishment. In the book *Black, Brilliant and Dyslexic*, editor Marcis Brisset-Bailey describes how, 'there may be a reluctance within sections of the black community to consider that children and adults may be dyslexic, as neurodiverse learning differences can be viewed as shameful, even as something that can be reversed by "hard work"'.[89]

For educators, the key message is that neurodivergence intersects with race and culture in ways that shape learners' opportunities, safety and confidence, and that awareness of this helps us create genuinely inclusive classrooms.

Age

Finally, depending on your teaching context, you may or may not find yourself working with older learners – people taking on a new language in their 50s, 60s, 70s (or above!). The number of diagnosed and self-identified neurodivergent people has been rising in recent years, but this does not mean that neurodivergent people themselves are becoming more common. Rather, due to increasing public awareness and changing diagnostic criteria, it means that more people are being recognised and accessing support, and that there is, therefore, a generation of older neurodivergent people who were not picked up when they were younger. There will, then, perhaps be older neurodivergent people in your classrooms who were never given the language to name and understand their differences.

Many of these people may also have been coerced into masking their differences. My own father, for example, educated in the UK in the 1960s, faced corporal punishment for writing with his left hand. As a

88 Nelson, T. (2024) *'Before people see the autism, they see my race': An intersectional exploration of the lived experiences of masking and camouflaging Black Autistic girls in UK education using IPA and DisCrit.* Doctoral dissertation, University of Essex & Tavistock and Portman NHS Foundation Trust.

89 Brissett-Bailey, M. (Ed.) (2023) *Black, Brilliant and Dyslexic: Neurodivergent heroes tell their stories.* Jessica Kingsley Publishers.

naturally left-handed person, whenever he reached for a pen with his left hand, it would be beaten with a wooden ruler by the teacher. Although left-handedness is not a form of neurodivergence per se, it *does* seem to be more common among neurodivergent individuals, and above all, it demonstrates how deviation from established norms often elicits a forceful attempt to try to 'correct' behaviour.

Older learners in your classroom may therefore not only carry undiagnosed neurodivergent traits, but also long histories of masking or being treated as having 'problem behaviour'. It's possible they might feel anxious about returning to education or have traumatic memories of past punishments or shaming. For some of these learners, formal qualifications may be lacking, unreflective of the skills they have and what they may be able to achieve with proper support and understanding.

Why intersectionality matters in ELT

Approaching neurodiversity through an intersectional lens helps us to notice how it is social structures – not individual learner's differences – that create barriers. For teachers, it reminds us that 'neurodivergent learner' is never a single, predictable category, and that many (*intersecting*) factors shape a learner's experiences and behaviour. A student who has ADHD and is non-binary, for example, may – especially in multicultural classrooms – face challenges around self-expression or classroom participation that are less about their language skills or cognitive profile. Likewise, a Black female autistic student may be carrying a heavy burden of social masking and codeswitching *on top* of trying to communicate in a second (*or third...*) language that could, at first glance, be misinterpreted as disinterest or having lower language levels.

For many English language teachers, this will feel like well-trodden ground. Reading nuanced social context is something we do every day, as is working sensitively with cultural difference and adapting communication to meet learners where they are. Bringing an intersectional lens to neurodiversity simply draws on those strengths and helps us to support learners to bring their full selves to the classroom. Beyond that, by fostering classroom cultures built on mutual respect, we help *all* our learners to develop the intercultural competence required to thrive in our multicultural world.

Decolonial perspectives on neurodivergence

An intersectional perspective also reminds us to reflect on whose experiences and voices are represented in the materials, studies and training we rely on. It's uncomfortable to acknowledge, but our field of English language teaching essentially grew out of the global spread of English as a colonial export; a history that continues to influence which experiences and knowledge traditions are foregrounded not only within ELT, but much more widely. The same dynamics of power and inequality also shape global medical paradigms and scientific research. Most relevant to our interests in this book, is that the vast majority of neurodiversity research – and neurodiversity theory, as we know it – has emerged from the Global North and the English-speaking world. This means we currently have only a partial picture of how cognitive, behavioural and sensory differences are understood in diverse cultural settings.

As we've already seen, many people are not represented in the statistics of diagnosed neurodivergence: diagnostic inequities exist in relation to race, age, gender, ethnicity, socioeconomic class, and many other intersections of a person's identity. But beyond this, there are cultural differences in how neurodivergence is thought about that often get sidelined when we approach the topic from the perspective of Western medicine and the Global North.[90] As teachers who regularly encounter learners from all walks of life and all kinds of cultural and linguistic backgrounds, it is all the more important for us to reflect on these alternative perspectives.

While the neurodiversity paradigm is generally understood as having its roots in the activism of online neurodivergent individuals in the 1990s, non-pathologising understandings of difference and neurodivergence have been present among various Global South, Indigenous and First People communities for far longer.[91] In some First Nation communities – including the Nipsihkipahk (Samson Cree Nation) in Canada – neurodivergence is thought of as a spiritual gift.[92] Similarly, within some West African precolonial traditions and philosophies, neurodivergent traits were viewed as unique abilities and afforded individuals important

90 Nair, V.K., Farah, W. & Boveda, M. (2024) Is neurodiversity a global northern white paradigm? *Autism*, p.13623613241280835.

91 Ibid.

92 Bruno, G. (2023) *The Gift of Being Different* [online]. Available at: https://vimeo.com/817471409 (accessed January 2026).

community roles such as 'healers, memory keepers, rhythm holders, energy workers, herbalists, and advisers'.[93] In both Māori and Sámi worldviews, too, difference is welcomed. Variation in health and in ways of being in the world are understood as being socially shaped rather than fixed individual traits.[94] It is also important, however, to remember that not all Global South, Indigenous and First People perspectives see neurodivergence in the same way. In some communities, there is far more stigma attached to neurodivergence, where it can be thought of as being the result of a curse or as placing a large burden on relatives.[95]

Global perspectives on neurodivergence

Because so much neurodiversity research is published in English-language speaking media, and based in Western and Global North contexts, there is limited accessible information about perspectives on neurodivergence in diverse cultural contexts. Of the published research that exists, the majority is focused on autism, with other minority neurotypes (like ADHD, dyslexia, dyspraxia, etc.) rarely receiving mention.

What we *can* say for certain, is that cultural norms will shape what is understood as neurotypical, and, in turn, what is a *divergence* from that. Similarly, while stigma around neurodivergence is commonplace, it will exist to a greater or lesser degree in different contexts and be influenced by local expectations. In China, for example, recent research has highlighted a limited understanding of autism as a medical diagnosis among the general population, but a high level of stigma – two factors that are probably linked.[96] Kieran Rose, autistic trainer and researcher, has observed the following:

- In some East Asian cultures, where social harmony and conformity may be highly valued, masking and suppressing expressions of neurodivergence is often expected. The pressure to adhere to rigid societal norms can be extreme, leading to internalised shame and burnout for many neurodivergent individuals.

93 Jallow, L. (2025) Neurodivergence Was Supported, Not Pathologized, *The Lovette Jallow Perspective* [online]. Available at: https://lovettejallow.substack.com/p/neurodivergence-ancient-africa (accessed January 2026).

94 Bortz, M.A. (2025) Introduction to the Forum: Embracing Neurodiversity: A Global Perspective. *Perspectives of the ASHA Special Interest Groups*, pp.1-6.

95 Ibid.

96 Yu, L., Stronach, S. & Harrison, A.J. (2020) Public knowledge and stigma of autism spectrum disorder: Comparing China with the United States. *Autism*, 24(6), pp.1531-1545.

- In Middle Eastern, African and South Asian societies, disability and neurodivergence may be tied to family honour. In some cases, neurodivergent individuals face concealment, lack of diagnosis, or limited access to support due to fears of social stigma impacting the entire family.
- In lower-income and postcolonial nations, economic survival may take precedence over accommodations, making formal diagnosis or any support services largely inaccessible to many neurodivergent people.[97]

In summary

Taking an intersectional and decolonial perspective helps us recognise that social and cultural factors have a large part to play both in how we think about neurodivergence (and neurotypicality) and in the lived experiences of neurodivergent individuals around the world. It also encourages us to reflect on our own assumptions and any stereotypes we may unintentionally carry into the classroom.

In this section, we've looked in depth at individual neurodivergent learners, from their unique communicative needs to intersectional aspects of their identities that may influence their experience of being neurodivergent and have a bearing on how they present in the classroom. In Section Four, we're going to transition to thinking specifically about teaching with neurodiversity in mind. In Chapter 7, we'll consider what language scaffolding neurodivergent English language learners may benefit from, to help them navigate communication outside of the classroom. In the final chapter, we'll walk through a set of practical suggestions – 'easy wins' – to help improve accessibility within your teaching.

97 Rose, K. (2024) What is Neurodiversity? [online]. *The Autistic Advocate*. Available at: https://theautisticadvocate.com/what-is-neurodiversity-new/ (accessed January 2026).

TL:DR (too long: didn't read) summary

- Neurodivergence rarely appears in neat categories. Many learners have multiple overlapping neurodivergences.
- New research is identifying brain-body connections in neurodivergence. We now know that neurodivergence often co-occurs with many physical conditions and differences, including chronic pain conditions, hypermobility, chronic fatigue and gastrointestinal issues. Neurodivergent learners may also need physical accommodations.
- *Intersectionality* – a term coined by Kimberlé Crenshaw – is the idea that different parts of a person's identity afford us different degrees of power or discrimination.
- A large portion of what we know about many minority neurotypes is biased and misses many *intersecting* perspectives and experiences. Women and girls, Black, Brown and racially minoritised individuals, as well as older people, are less likely to receive diagnoses and support and are more likely to face additional discriminations.
- Global North and English-speaking perspectives dominate our current understanding of neurodivergence. As such, we only have a partial picture of global perspectives, with much of what we do know mostly focused on autism.
- Cultural perspectives on neurodivergence vary widely. Some cultures celebrate neurodivergence, others attach stigma. Teachers need to be aware of the potential for cultural differences in how learners may feel about their own – or their classmates' – neurodivergence.

Reflective questions

1. Which aspects of your own identity lend you privilege in educational spaces, and which might make you feel more vulnerable?
2. How might your own intersectional identity shape the way you read learners' behaviour?
3. In your typical teaching context, how might a neurodivergent learner's experiences of race, gender, religion or age influence whether they feel comfortable disclosing their needs?
4. What are the typical cultural views on neurodiversity in your current teaching context? How might you find out more about this, if you're currently unsure?

Section Four

Teaching for Neurodiversity

Chapter 7: Supporting neurodivergent language learners beyond the classroom

By the end of this chapter you'll be able to:

- recognise how meaning is often dependent on context
- describe the difference between semantic and pragmatics
- identify the importance of pragmatic competence in L2 (second language) contexts, in particular for neurodivergent learners
- plan and deliver pragmatic awareness-raising activities that are appropriate to your learners.

In this final section, we'll think more closely about what it means to *teach for neurodiversity* in practical terms. In the previous sections, we've covered the foundations: the core principles of neurodiversity; inclusive teaching and our responsibilities as educators; and the unique needs of neurodivergent learners. We've also begun (in Chapter 5) to explore the broader communicative profiles of neurodivergent learners, using ideas like the Double Empathy Problem, monotropism and gestalt learning to help us reframe neurodivergent communicative differences.

This chapter begins Section Four by taking our interest in neurodivergent communication further still. Here, we'll focus on the role of the language teacher and reflect on what we may need to explicitly teach in order to meet the specific linguistic and *pragmatic* needs of neurodivergent individuals navigating L2 (second-language) contexts.

Second language users in a neurodiverse world

As language teachers, our aims are usually to equip and support learners to use English as a second (or third) language as a tool for navigating the world around them. Students usually *need* English to *do* something: whether that be to consume English-language media, to travel, to mediate work encounters or to move through everyday life in an English-dominant country. Whatever their motivation for learning English, as soon as they take it beyond the textbook in a classroom, language becomes alive in the context of interaction.[98]

Even within first language (L1) encounters, communication is rarely perfectly predictable (or perfectly successful). Words, phrases and expressions take on new meanings with new use and in multilingual and multicultural L2 settings, these challenges are amplified. Within L1 interactions, neurodivergent speakers are often at a disadvantage – experiencing a Double Empathy Problem gap in mutual understanding that is usually interpreted as the neurodivergent communicator's responsibility (or 'failure'). For neurodivergent individuals communicating in L2 contexts, the scope for misunderstanding or misunderstanding can sometimes be far greater,[99] creating a kind of *double*-Double Empathy Problem.[100]

Teaching for neurodiversity involves thinking beyond classroom adjustments and accommodations (although these, of course, are essential) towards the interactional work learners are expected to do outside the classroom, in everyday contexts. We need to equip learners with the tools they require to navigate potential communicative breakdowns, to pre-empt them, and to manage rapport as well as repair.

98 Often, of course, the classroom is a microcosm of the 'outside world' and the same issues are just as likely to arise within the classroom as without.

99 However, see the 'In Focus: Neurodivergent teachers' box on page 129 for examples of how being an L2 neurodivergent speaker can also sometimes reduce barriers…

100 A 'Double Empathy Problem (squared)'?

To do this, we can turn to the linguistic field of *pragmatics*: the sub-field of linguistics (the study of language and communication) that interests itself in communication *in context*. The following chapter explores how we can prepare neurodivergent learners for these unique demands, and how *pragmatic* competence can be taught and fostered in ways that support learners' communicative autonomy and confidence.

Pragmatics and pragmatic competence

Often, what we say is not what we mean. Imagine the following scenario: there's been a long staff meeting during a lunch break during which the Director of Studies has delivered an incredibly boring PowerPoint presentation about the new marketing plan for the language school. The next day, a colleague who missed the meeting asks you how it was. Your answer? 'Fantastic…' (with a forced smile and one eyebrow raised).

Utterances (i.e. things people say, not necessarily full sentences) are often unclear. There are many different reasons for fuzziness in meaning that can take place at any level of language: from *ambiguity* at a word level (for example, 'I'm going down to the **bank**' – here 'bank' could refer to both a financial institution or the side of a river), to something often referred to as *indeterminacy* (i.e. vagueness) at a word or sentence level.

Indeterminacy arises when the words themselves are not sufficient to fully convey the intended meaning. In our example above, the answer 'fantastic' in response to a colleague's question, on face value, means it was a brilliant, a remarkable talk. However, we know that the talk *was not* brilliant or remarkable, and the speaker intends their colleague to draw this non-dictionary-definition meaning from what they say. This difference between what is said and what is meant lies at the heart of the distinction between *semantics* and *pragmatics*. In ELT – particularly when working with lower-level learners – our focus is often on semantic meaning: the kind you'll find recorded in a dictionary.

Coded and inferred meaning

When we communicate, we draw on both *coded* and *inferred* meaning. Coded meaning closely overlaps with what we tend to think of as *semantic* meaning: the information that is explicitly encoded in words and grammatical structures within a shared linguistic system. For instance, when a teacher says, 'Open your books to page ten', the coded meaning is clear: learners are being instructed to perform a specific action, finding a specific page. Much of the language we focus on in ELT classrooms works in this way. Vocabulary items and grammatical forms are conventionally paired with meanings, which is why they can be recorded in dictionaries, taught, practised and assessed. As long as speakers and listeners share the same code (i.e. the language, as recorded), understanding is largely straightforward.

However, human communication rarely stops at what is explicitly encoded. In everyday interactions, we often use context to work out what a speaker really means. This involves drawing on information beyond the words themselves in order to infer the speaker's intended meaning (known as an *implicature*). In terms of the 'fantastic' example above, context used by the hearer may include the shared knowledge that lunchtime meetings are usually a drag, alongside cues such as the speaker's forced smile, to recognise that the comment is not meant literally.

Figure 7.1: A graphic image of a Brown woman sat on a chair saying the words 'It's a bit chilly'. In a box next to her, text reads: 'Potential speaker meanings: I'm cold; Could I borrow a jumper/blanket?; Would you mind lighting the fire?; It's time for me/us to leave; Come sit closer and put your arm around me'.

Another example I often like to use when I'm talking about this, is the utterance 'It's getting a little bit chilly'. On the surface – and how we might teach this slightly colloquial expression as a lexical chunk – the meaning is clear: the speaker is telling us she is feeling or noticing the cold. Yet, in slightly different circumstances (with slightly different contextual cues), the *intended speaker meaning* could be very different. For instance, spoken to a close friend or family member at the beginning of a visit to their home, the *implicature* might be that they are requesting to borrow a jumper or a blanket to warm up. Likewise, it might be meant to indicate that the speaker would like to close a window, or hint that the listener might light a fire or turn the central heating on. At the end of a long day or night out, it might represent a cue to leave. Directed towards a partner or romantic interest, it might be an invitation to snuggle up...

What's clear is that meaning is often shaped by context. Miraculously, in most cases, we seem to be very good at inferring a speaker's intended meaning. However, there are also many occasions when it takes several attempts for us to get it right. To illustrate this, let's take a look at a couple of examples from the longstanding BBC Radio 4 agricultural drama *The Archers* (because I am an *Archers* mega-fan and, as we saw in Chapter 5, you can get the best out of neurodivergent people when your harness their interests). Consider this first exchange between Susan Carter and her brother Clive in the vegetable aisle of a local grocery shop:

> **Susan:** Clive! What are you *doing* here?
>
> **Clive:** A bit of shopping for my tea.[101]

As an isolated extract this response makes perfect sense – I'm here, in the grocery shop, to pick up some food to have for my tea (aka 'supper' or 'dinner'). However, in the wider context, that Clive has long been estranged from his sister Susan and no longer lives in the village, we can see that what Susan was really asking was – what are you doing back in the village (not in this grocery store).

In this case, the misunderstanding hinges on something called *deixis* – the way words like *here*, *there*, *now* and *you* 'point' to something specific in context. Deictic expressions pick out part of a wider situation. However, *which* exact part they indicate can only be worked out by interpreting the

101 *The Archers*, BBC Radio 4. Episode first broadcast 26/08/2024.

speaker's perspective and intentions. Clive hears 'here' as meaning 'this grocery shop' but Susan's intended 'here' was really 'back in the village'. The word is the same, but the meaning is different.

Deixis is just one example of how context-dependent language can introduce indeterminacy (and the risk for misunderstanding) in communication. In the second extract from a different episode of *The Archers*, we see a slightly different kind of misunderstanding unfold.[102] Here, Ed Grundy is chatting to Brad Horrobin about Ed's step-son George, who's just recently come home from a year in prison:

> **Ed:** I've never seen [George] this low […]. I did wonder about doing something later, though, try and cheer him up.
>
> **Brad:** Good idea.
>
> **Ed:** Wondering about bowling?
>
> **Brad:** Bowling?
>
> **Ed:** Yeah, I know it might seem a bit naff, but George used to really love it and it might distract him for an hour or so? What do you think?
>
> **Brad:** I think he'll like it, yeah.
>
> **Ed:** No, no I mean – if we go tonight do you wanna come?

In this example, the misunderstanding arises from an ambiguity about what 'bowling' is referring to in the conversation. Brad infers that Ed is talking about taking George bowling, and asking for Brad's opinion on whether he thinks this will help cheer George up. In fact, Ed is trying to signal an invitation to Brad to come along, too. In this instance, there's both a kind of *referential* ambiguity here (in terms of what is being referred to by 'bowling'), but there's also a *speech-act* issue. Because invitations are often phrased indirectly, it's easy for listeners to miss that an invitation is even happening.

If terms like *speech act*, *deixis*, *referents*, and *implicature* all feel a little alien, don't worry – it's not necessary for you to become an expert in pragmatics for you to be in a position to nurture the pragmatic competence of your learners. What's important is simply the understanding that mis- (or non-)understandings often have a pragmatic basis: there's often some kind of mismatch in expectations

102 *The Archers*, BBC Radio 4. Episode first broadcast 04/12/2025.

and assumptions about shared context. Between speakers of the same language (and same neurotype), these are often very repairable – we rephrase, ask for clarification, signal confusion, laugh or employ a great many other strategies to realign understanding. In communication that takes places with fewer shared resources – such as between speakers of different language backgrounds, or with different neurotypes – this can often be a little more effortful, and learners may need our support in developing the skills to navigate these moments.

Pragmatic competence, neurodivergence and second-language learning

Most English-language teaching tends to prioritise semantic meaning over speaker meaning (i.e. the meanings of words and sentences as they are recorded and taught, rather than what speakers intend when they use them). In the ELT classroom – at least from my experience – it is uncommon to address the fact that, when we say something, when we use language: we are usually inviting inferences. Alongside the four skills (reading, writing, listening and speaking), coursebooks tend to divide their focus between vocabulary, grammar and pronunciation. Some also prioritise *functional language* (for example, phrases or expressions that fulfil a specific purpose, like asking for advice, making requests, offering suggestions or disagreeing). Yet despite its importance for our ability to understanding speaker meaning – and to make ourselves well understood – the pragmatic aspects of language are rarely addressed explicitly in ELT.

This feels like something of an oversight when it comes to properly equipping our learners to use English as a second language to navigate the world. As we've seen, words and phrases will mean different things in different contexts. In order to correctly infer an intended speaker meaning (or *implicature*), we need to draw on context to enrich our interpretations. Yet our understanding of 'context' is heavily reliant on our *assumptions* about what we, as speakers, share in a given moment: assumptions about shared knowledge, shared norms, shared cultural expectations and often a shared environment. In L2 interactions (that are also often cross-cultural), where many of the above are *not* shared, the opportunity for misunderstanding is a lot greater. Learners need both awareness of this shared context gap, and the tools to enable them to negotiate real-world language use that is often slippery or loose.

For neurodivergent L2 users, this is even more important. In first-language contexts, cross-neurotype communication often faces additional challenges. We saw this earlier, in Chapter 5, when we encountered the Double Empathy Problem and the difficulties that neurodivergent and neurotypical people often have in understanding one another. Refracted through the further lenses of language and cultural difference that L2 speakers already experience, neurodivergent L2 learners face a kind of *double*-Double Empathy Problem, with more opportunities for misunderstanding to arise.

By way of example, in the UK, it is common to speak indirectly in polite conversation, conveying intended meaning through hints and suggestion (just like Ed and his vague invite to go bowling).

This has given rise to a popular meme in neurodivergent online spaces that goes something like this image below:

Figure 7.2: A meme with a 1950s-style graphic illustration of a white man in a beige shirt smiling directly to camera against a blue background. Text reads: 'Look at me I'm a neurotypical. I give weird hints about things instead of just telling people...'

In various versions of the meme, a smug or proud face is shown next to the caption 'Look at me I'm neurotypical. I give weird hints about things instead of just telling people...'[103] The humour lies in playful inversion of the medical model perspective (from Chapter 1) that neurodivergent people have impaired communication – in particular in relation to the autistic preference for direct, explicit communication. Here, it is indirectness, vagueness and reliance on unspoken cues that are presented as the communicative problem.[104]

Pragmatic competence is an essential component of language use, but one that is often overlooked in ELT and second-language instruction. For the neurodivergent learners we encounter in the English language classroom, development of their pragmatic skills is all the more imperative. For all learners, the ability to smoothly navigate the inevitable pragmatic misunderstandings in a second (or third) language will set them up to become effective and confident communicators, no matter their level of English. For neurodivergent learners – who are already at something of a disadvantage in an L1 – it can be a linguistic lifeline.

Fostering pragmatic competence in the ELT classroom

The first step in supporting learners to develop their pragmatic competence is to raise their awareness of the difference between semantic and pragmatic meanings and the crucial role of context in the different ways an utterance can be interpreted. Learners need to understand that the dictionary meaning of words often isn't enough to fully grasp what a speaker intends.

There are many ways to do this in the classroom. One effective approach in monolingual groups is to use the learners' L1 as a reference point to compare how things like politeness, indirectness, implicature and ambiguity function in different or similar ways. The opportunities really are endless. But, to get you started, in the box below, you'll find three suggested activities that you can adapt to your teaching context that encourage learners to notice, reflect on and practise using context to guide meaning.

103 My neurotypical exemplar for this meme is knowingly close the mythical norm...

104 As an autistic person, I'm inclined to agree!

Activities for raising pragmatic awareness

(Adapted from Peter Grundy (2013) *Doing Pragmatics*)

Sensitising your learners to the role of context in utterance interpretation can help support the development of their pragmatic competence. The following activities provide a gentle way into this and can be slotted into lessons or courses as engaging fillers and add-ons.

Activity 1: Guess the context

Task learners to work alone or in pairs to script a short dialogue between two imaginary characters. In small groups, ask learners to read aloud or show their scripts. Learners take it in turns to guess the context of the conversation, then discuss. If undertaken in English, this activity is more suitable for intermediate learners and above. However, it doesn't necessarily need to be completed in English. For lower-level learners, consider using translanguaging.

Activity 2: How many meanings?

The aim of this activity is to encourage learners to recognise how meaning can vary depending on context. You can set this activity up in a number of different ways – for example, gamified, alone or in groups, extended into improvised role plays – depending on the makeup of your class or learners, etc. Provide learners the following utterances: *I'm tired*; *I'm sorry*; *It's me*; *I thought so*; *Don't*. Next, ask them to brainstorm all the different contexts that these might be used. A follow-up discussion question can be posed, asking learners why they think a single utterance can be used as so many different speech acts, or in so many different functional ways.

Activity 3: Pitch(ure) perfect

This activity is great for learners who enjoy visual cues. As with the activities above, you can set it up in a number of ways – as homework or on rotating stations around the classroom; you could ask learners to work alone or in pairs to write their own answers then feed back as a group, or ask learners to write their answers under the pictures.

First, choose a small number of interesting images from a magazine or newspaper featuring different characters (for example, a couple in the middle of a marriage proposal, a burglar, a small child, etc.). Next, write a communicative instruction for each image that the learners must craft. For example, 'Ask these two for directions', or 'Get this person to call you mummy', or 'Ask this person for their bag', etc. As learners become more familiar with the activity and the process of pragmatically pitching utterances, you can make your instructions sillier or more challenging.

Once learners have been sensitised to these different layers of meaning, the second step is to provide them with the tools needed to navigate pragmatic misunderstandings. These tools will help learners anticipate and repair communication breakdowns in real-world interactions.

Both pre-emptive and remediation strategies can be used to prevent misunderstanding, and it is useful for students to learn and practice both. Research on interaction shows that speakers and listeners do not simply wait for communication to break down before acting. Instead, they often work actively to prevent or repair misunderstandings as they arise. Speakers may do this by repeating or reformulating what they have said, checking comprehension, adding explanations, or making their intended meaning more explicit. Listeners, meanwhile, are not passive recipients. When understanding is uncertain, they may initiate negotiation work by asking for clarification or confirmation, rather than simply 'letting it pass'.

Importantly, difficulty in understanding is not always signalled verbally. In interaction, listeners may also display subtle non-verbal cues (such as pauses or momentary stillness), which teachers and learners may recognise from everyday communicative experience as indicating that meaning has not yet been fully grasped. Once understanding is restored, interaction often becomes more fluid again. Raising learners' awareness of these speaker and listener strategies, as well as the verbal and non-verbal signs that misunderstanding may be occurring, can help equip them with practical tools for navigating cross-cultural, cross-neurotype L2 interactions more confidently and effectively.

The following table illustrates a range of speaker and listener strategies identified by McDonough *et al* in a study of L2 interaction at a Canadian university.[105] While not exhaustive, these examples show how speakers and listeners actively work to prevent and repair misunderstanding in real-time conversation.

105 McDonough, K., Liu, C. & Trofimovich, P. (2023) Strategies for avoiding misunderstanding in English L2 conversations. *ELT Journal*, 77(4): 426-434.

Who?	Category	Definition	Example
Speaker	**Comprehension check**	Speaker asks whether listener has understood.	***'You know what I mean?'***
Speaker	**Self-repair**	Speaker modifies part of their utterance.	'200 dollars to buy uh um***, I'm sorry, 2,000 dollars.'***
Speaker	**Elaboration**	Speaker provides additional information, such as giving examples or specifying the meaning of a word or phrase.	'One day if I come across someone ***like just if I'm shopping outside*** I'm talking to the cashier.'
Listener	**Confirmation check**	Listener checks understanding by repeating something the speaker said, may occur with rising intonation or *do you mean.*	Speaker: 'In Korea, everything is different than here.' Listener: 'Right.' Speaker: 'Eventually you like it actually.' Listener: '***You like it?'*** Speaker: 'Yeah starting out it was confusing but eventually you will enjoy the food and the people.'

Listener	**Clarification request**	Listener asks speaker to clarify through an open-ended or specific request, or an or-choice question.	Speaker: 'You moved here with your parents?' Listener: ***'Sorry?'*** Speaker: 'You moved with your parents from China?' Listener: 'Uh, they are still in China.'

Together, these strategies can be made visible and learnable through classroom activities that encourage noticing and guided practice. This might involve drawing learners' attention to the functional language typically used to check understanding, request clarification or reformulate meaning, and giving them opportunities to rehearse these moves in low-stakes interaction. Such work can be supported through exposure to authentic language use, for example by drawing on L2 or ELF (English as a lingua franca) corpora, analysing short video clips of real-life meaning negotiation, or engaging with unsanitised examples of spoken interaction rather than idealised textbook dialogue. In this way, pragmatic competence becomes something learners can actively practise, rather than something they are expected to acquire implicitly.

In summary

Raising the pragmatic competence of our learners is especially useful for those who are neurodivergent and facing a potentially *double-*Double Empathy Problem: as it equips them to navigate inevitable misunderstandings with confidence. This work is not about enforcing neurotypical norms, but about giving learners awareness, strategies, and choice in how they navigate interaction.

However, as with many reasonable adjustments or accommodations, there is often a 'curb-cut' effect that ultimately benefits all. It is not only your neurodivergent learners who will need to navigate a neurodiverse world. Neurotypical learners will undoubtedly find themselves using their English with neurodivergent L1 and L2 English speakers, as well as with L2 language users from different cultures and backgrounds, with different L2 English competencies. By supporting learners to strengthen their pragmatic competence we are, at the same time, helping them to develop their *intercultural communicative competence* – their ability to navigate a world of difference – which, in a deeply interconnected, globalised world, feels like an important skill to foster.

In the coming, final chapter, we'll think about practical adjustments you can make to your planning and teaching to improve accessibility for all...

TL:DR (too long: didn't read) summary

- The meanings of words and *utterances* (things that people say) are not as fixed as they first may seem. Often, we need to *infer* a speaker's intended meaning (an *implicature*) by drawing on context (for example, shared knowledge, local norms, body language or situational cues).
- *Pragmatics* is the sub-field of linguistics that deals with speaker meaning (in contrast to *semantics* which deals with encoded, dictionary-definition meanings).
- Misunderstandings and communication ruptures often occur at the pragmatic level (i.e. in relation to speaker intended meaning) yet pragmatic awareness is under-taught in EFL.
- Fostering pragmatic competence can be helpful for *all* second-language learners, but particularly so for those who are neurodivergent, as they face a potentially *double*-Double Empathy Problem – in other words, navigating both cross-neurotype and cross-cultural gaps, often with still developing language resources.
- You can use a two-step process to develop your learners' pragmatic competence. The first step involves activities to raise learners' awareness of differences between pragmatic and semantic meanings, and the importance of context in utterance interpretation.
- The second step involves making pragmatic strategies (such as comprehension checks and clarification requests) visible and learnable through low-stakes exercises, use of authentic language (video clips, corpora, unsanitised dialogue) and guided practice.

Reflective questions

1. Thinking about interactions that have taken place in your first language, can you recall any moments when you've misjudged a speaker's implicature (intended meaning) or a listener has misjudged yours? How did you repair the rupture in understanding?
2. Can you think of any similar instances that have occurred in your second (or third) language? What made this easier or harder to navigate?
3. How familiar or unfamiliar is thinking about pragmatic competence in the ELT classroom? What one small thing could you do to make it more comfortable for you, or more explicit for your learners?

Chapter 8: Accessibility for all

By the end of this chapter you'll be able to:

- plan inclusive lessons that support a range of neurodivergent learners to participate fully
- be more aware of neurodivergent teaching colleagues and how you might best support them.

The aim of this final chapter is to offer practical suggestions for reasonable adjustments and accessibility accommodations that you can make to your teaching, assessment and classroom environments to help support the various needs of different neurodivergent learners. As has been the case throughout this book, this is not an exhaustive list of changes you can make to improve accessibility. My hope is that it will function more as a set of launch points for your own reflections on what might benefit your learners, in your own, unique teaching contexts.

As we saw in Chapter 4, many of the most helpful and effective changes you can make are those that fit within the UDL approach of offering choice and flexibility in methods of engagement (with learning), representation (of learning materials and information) and action and expression (for example, flexible and varied approaches to assessment). By building flexibility in from the start, the need to provide bespoke reasonable adjustments for multiple learners is reduced – saving teacher time and increasing accessibility for all. At the end of this book, there are a number of reflective tools that can guide you to identify what UDL-style changes might be required or easily actioned in your current teaching setup.

That said, there will, on occasion, be more specific needs that individual neurodivergent learners have that may need to be accommodated separately. This chapter hopes to offer you a starting menu of suggestions for suitable adjustments for different potential learners needs. Because barriers to learning often arise from how physical and teaching environments are designed and organised (rather than from learners themselves) the practical suggestions in this chapter are organised by areas of access rather than by neurodivergent diagnoses.

As always, it is important to remember that reasonable adjustments should be person-centred and guided by the individual learner. Neurodivergent learners are not all the same and what supports one learner may not work well for another. At the same time, not all learners will wish to talk about neurodivergence, disclose a diagnosis, or even see themselves in these terms. As teachers, we need to be careful not to make assumptions or force conversations: instead focusing on creating environments in which learners can choose to share what helps them, if and when they feel comfortable.

Finally, this chapter is titled 'Accessibility for all' because the aim really is to make English language learning as accessible as possible for everyone involved. A theme that has run throughout this book is the idea that, when you make accessibility changes for some, they usually benefit all (as with the 'curb-cut' effect discussed in Chapter 4). Many of the suggestions in the following pages may benefit learners who consider themselves to be neurotypical as well as neurodivergent learners, with or without formal diagnoses. However, learners are not the only people in the English language classroom who may be neurodivergent; teachers are just as likely to be neurodivergent. In fact, the language teaching profession may be one that is especially suited to many neurodivergent individuals. Reasonable adjustments and accessibility accommodations adopted in the classroom can benefit everyone who engages with them – both learners and teachers.

In focus: Neurodivergent teachers

So far in this book we have focused on the needs of neurodivergent learners. Yet neurodivergent people often make strong teachers. As we saw in Chapter 2, being neurodivergent often brings unique strengths that are incredibly valuable for teaching professions: such as heightened empathy and interpersonal skills, creativity, resilience and attention to detail. When it comes to ELT – a profession that draws on detailed expertise in language systems alongside a drive to support and nurture others – it may be especially appealing.

In her essay *Why teaching English as a second language makes me feel known*, Australian autistic writer and EFL teacher Adele Dumont describes how the role of 'language teacher' felt easy to slip into.[106] From the moment she began her initial training, she describes feeling far more at ease in the classroom (with its defined and structured rules of engagement) than in the staffroom at breaktimes where social interaction was less predictable and her social role less clear.

For those who have found it hard to make themselves understood in their first language, or who have faced stigma for being perceived as 'different', cross-cultural interactions – such as those you might experience while living abroad or working in EFL – can also offer an interesting freedom. For example, reflecting on their experience as an autistic bilingual American abroad, Alyssa Hillary observed that the Double Empathy Problem 'was less of a problem for me in China, despite the greater difference in perspectives, because principles of cross-cultural communication were used over the idea that *I have a communication disorder, so this is my problem*'.[107]

I, too, had similar experiences when living in Sardinia in my early 20s and working in a bar with very early intermediate level Italian as my only means of communicating. In the UK, as a (then undiagnosed) neurodivergent young person, social interaction had often felt fraught and rife with misunderstanding. In contrast, communicating via a limited

106 hapter in Bastow, C. & Case, J. (Eds.) (2025) *Someone Like Me: An anthology of non-fiction by autistic writers.*

107 Hillary, A. (2020) Autist/biography. In: *The Palgrave Handbook of Auto/biography* (pp. 315-339). Cham: Springer International Publishing.

second language, mutual understanding seemed easier to reach: perhaps because of the forgiveness that is often given to second-language users by native speakers. In some ways, the smaller the shared linguistic and cultural repertoire, the easier it can be to skim over the more nuanced details that often trip up cross-neurotype communication within a shared first language.

Just as with neurodivergent learners, neurodivergent teaching colleagues may mask their neurodivergent traits in the workplace or fear stigma or judgement, all of which can increase pressures and the risk of burnout. In addition to offering kindness and collegial support to neurodivergent colleagues, we can extend to them the same kind of reasonable adjustments and accommodations that we do to learners – things like adapting the sensory environment or respecting quiet moments, providing clear handover instructions, facilitating choice and flexibility in how lessons are delivered, providing closed captions on video training materials and video conferencing meetings, or offering differently coloured paper for print-outs...

Improving access to the learning environment

The learning environment plays an important role in shaping how easily learners are able to engage with and participate in classroom activities. Across many minority neurotypes, sensory processing and sensory experiences can differ from those of neurotypical individuals, meaning that aspects such as noise and lighting levels can be experienced as either enabling or disabling. Visual features of the classroom and learning materials – including layout, font choice, spacing and colour – can also significantly affect how easily information is processed by some learners. In increasingly blended and digital learning contexts, accessibility is further shaped by the design of online platforms, digital documents and multimedia resources.

Together, small changes across these sensory, visual and digital aspects of the learning environment can reduce unnecessary cognitive effort, freeing up space for learners to engage more comfortably with learning.

Sensory access

Sensory aspects of the classroom environment (such as light and noise levels, visual clutter, colour palettes, opportunities for movement and rest and tactile features of classroom furniture) can significantly affect learners' ability to regulate their attention and engage with learning. Importantly, while for some neurodivergent learners, environments that are noisy, bright, visually busy or unpredictable can be particularly taxing, others may actively benefit from movement, tactile input or changes in sensory stimulation in order to stay regulated and focused. As ever, offering choice is often more effective than enforcing uniform conditions.

Sensory access: Some practical adjustments

- **Be mindful of sensory stimulation in the classroom:** This might include avoiding over-bright or flickering lights where possible, reducing background noise during key moments such as when giving instructions or during listening activities, minimising strong smells (like perfumes or bleach) and keeping notice boards or white boards tidy and focused around the task at hand. Where features of the physical environment can't be changed (for example, strip lighting), allow learners to make themselves more comfortable by wearing hats or sunglasses, etc.
- **Offer options for sensory input and management:** Where possible, provide quieter working options alongside more interactive activities or stations, and be mindful of background noise during instructions or listening tasks. Some learners may benefit from using 'stim toys' (for example, fidget spinners or squeeze balls) to help them focus. Where possible, this should be supported as long as any incidental noise (for example, from a clicking toy) doesn't distract or distress other learners.
- **Build in opportunities for movement:** Allowing learners to change position, stand, stretch or move discreetly can support regulation, particularly for learners who seek sensory input to maintain focus and regulation.

Visual access

For all of us, the way materials look on the page or screen has a real impact on how easy they are to read and understand. For some neurodivergent people, this impact can be disabling, creating significant barriers to access. Features such as layout, spacing, font choice and colour contrast can either support processing or make it harder, particularly for learners with dyslexia, visual stress or low vision. Clear, uncluttered materials tend to help everyone, while busy layouts or low contrast can add unnecessary effort.

In focus: Accessible fonts and layout

In general, accessible text tends to have:

- clear, distinguishable letter forms – for example, it's easy to differentiate between 'I' (capital i), 'l' (lower case L) and '1' (number one)
- good spacing – for example, 'rn' does not look like 'm'
- strong contrast between text and background.

Sans-serif fonts are often easier to read than serif fonts. Commonly recommended options include Arial, Calibri, Helvetica, Open Sans and Verdana. Fonts with decorative or dense letterforms (such as Times New Roman or Garamond) may be harder to process for some learners.

Other supportive strategies may include:

- using larger font sizes (12pt minimum)
- avoiding busy backgrounds or bright patterns
- making using of plain space and blocking text
- using bold for emphasis rather than italics
- using off-white paper and backgrounds as standard, and offering alternative coloured paper or background options where helpful.

Digital access

As learning increasingly takes place across digital platforms, accessibility is also shaped by the design of online materials. This has recently been reinforced through the EU Accessibility Act (EAA), which places greater emphasis on the accessibility of digital content. Simple features such as closed captions (i.e. subtitles) on video materials, alt text for images and clearly structured slides (including minimal text, consistent layouts and high visual contrast) can significantly improve access for neurodivergent learners, as well as for learners using assistive technologies.

Wherever possible, providing digital materials in advance or in downloadable formats can also help learners engage with content at their own pace.

In focus: Alt text

Alt text (short for *alternative text*) is a brief written description of an image that is read aloud by screen readers or displayed when images cannot be viewed. Its purpose is to convey the essential information or meaning of an image to learners who cannot access it visually.

Good alt text focuses on what matters for understanding and learning. This can also include socially meaningful visual information, such as race, gender presentation, disability, age or setting. For example, alt text for a photo used to illustrate turn-taking in conversation might describe the fact that this is a photo (and not a graphic design), who is interacting, how they are positioned, and what the interaction shows.

Improving access to instructions and tasks

The ways in which instructions and tasks are designed directly influence how accessible learning feels to different learners. For many neurodivergent learners, learning aims that might otherwise be very achievable can be made inaccessible by difficulties in how instructions are phrased or sequenced, particularly when expectations are implicit or imprecise.

Language can also create hidden barriers. Ambiguity, idiomatic expressions or dense spoken input can increase cognitive demand, even when learners have a high level of English. By adjusting both how instructions are framed and the language we use to deliver them, we can give learners a better chance of understanding how they can best engage with activities.

Access to instructions and tasks: Some practical adjustments

- **Provide instructions both verbally and in writing:** This allows learners to revisit information at their own pace and reduces reliance on real-time processing.

- **Use clear, concrete timeframes and deadlines:** Avoid vague phrases such as 'a few minutes' and instead specify how long tasks will take and when they will end. You could even write the time for an activity on the board as a point of reference.
- **Make success criteria explicit:** Clearly explain what learners are expected to produce and what a completed task should look like. Where possible, share examples of successful and unsuccessful outcomes.
- **Be mindful of processing speed as distinct from language ability:** Some learners may understand English well but need more time to process instructions or organise a response.
- **Build in permission to ask questions and seek clarification:** Normalising clarification reduces anxiety and helps prevent misunderstandings from becoming barriers to participation.
- **Plan for breaks and make them predictable:** Let learners know well in advance when breaks are scheduled and, where possible, stick to them to support regulation and sustained engagement. For some learners, a pre-break activity over-running by five minutes will go unnoticed, but for others this could be a huge source of stress.
- **Be prepared to rephrase or restate instructions:** Keep the Double Empathy Problem in mind – you may need to rethink how you explain a language point or deliver instructions. Your way of understanding something may not necessarily match that of your learners.

Language access: Minimising hidden linguistic barriers

- **Be aware of idiomatic and ambiguous language:** For learners whose goals include engaging with native-speaker norms, exposure to idiomatic language can be valuable. However, idioms and indirect meanings can significantly increase cognitive demand, even for learners with strong grammatical knowledge. Being judicious about when (and when not) to include this kind of language can help reduce unnecessary barriers to understanding.
- **Treat phrasal verbs as discrete vocabulary items:** Many phrasal verbs are not easily deduced from their parts and may need to be learned, practised and revisited individually.
- **Limit unnecessary filler words in instructions:** Words such as 'just', 'basically' or 'kind of' can make spoken input harder to process, particularly in fast-paced explanations and for lower-level learners.

- **Model and practise clarification strategies:** Explicitly teaching how to ask for repetition, rephrasing or examples supports learners to repair breakdowns in understanding.

Aa Terminology note: Avoiding pathologising or stigmatising language

Language choices shape how safe and understood learners feel in the classroom. The language used to describe difficulties, disability or difference can sometimes create additional barriers to participation if it makes learners feel judged or dehumanised.

In practice, openness, kindness and curiosity usually matter far more than perfect terminology. However, the following principles can be a helpful guide:

- **Preferences vary:** There is no single set of terms that *all* neurodivergent people agree on. Some learners may describe themselves as disabled, while others may not, and some may not use neurodiversity-related language at all. Where possible, listen to the language learners use for themselves and follow their lead.
- **Avoid inherently negative or deficit-focused phrasing:** Expressions such as '*suffers from*' frame difference as harm or tragedy and can be distancing or experienced as stigmatising.
- **Be cautious with language that minimises difficulty:** Phrases like 'We're all a bit ADHD' or 'Everyone's on the spectrum' are often intended empathetically but can unintentionally downplay the very real challenges some learners experience.
- **If in doubt, it can be helpful to reflect on whether the language being used aligns with the social model of disability:** This emphasises that barriers arise from environments and systems, rather than from individuals themselves. Language that focuses on access, support and flexibility is more likely to foster inclusion than language that centres deficit or limitation.

Improving access to sustained engagement

As we explored in Chapter 5, attention allocation and the ability to focus is something that can be experienced quite differently by some neurodivergent people. In some cases, deep flow states and heightened attention can supercharge learning while in others, focus can feel fleeting or scattered, and certainly hard to harness. As teachers, we have a lot of scope in how we can either support or hinder learners in their ability to sustain focus and engagement.

Competing demands on attention can make it difficult for some learners to maintain focus, particularly when environments are unpredictable or overstimulating. By adapting aspects of the learning and sensory environments, as suggested above, we can already begin to reduce some of the unnecessary cognitive demands on learners. The following, additional adjustments can assist in supporting regulation and sustained engagement.

Supporting sustained engagement: Some practical adjustments

- **Pace lessons and chunk tasks into manageable stages:** Breaking activities into clear steps can help learners maintain focus without becoming overwhelmed.
- **Build in regular breaks and task variation:** Short pauses or changes in activity can support regulation and help learners re-engage, particularly during longer lessons.
- **Allow sufficient processing time:** Some learners may need extra time to think, plan or, importantly, transition between tasks, even when they are fully engaged.
- **Respect quiet or low-output moments:** Periods of listening, thinking or reduced visible participation can still reflect meaningful engagement.
- **Offer autonomy where possible:** Choice over task order, format or working style can support self-regulation and sustained attention.
- **Draw on learners' interests and strengths:** Connecting tasks to learners' existing interests or talents can increase motivation and support deeper focus, particularly for learners with monotropic attention styles.
- **Make the purpose of activities explicit and support transitions:** Clearly explaining why an activity is being done, and allowing a brief transition period before a new task, can help learners engage more comfortably.

Improving access to interaction and participation

Because we are part of classroom culture every day, it can be easy to become acclimatised to the rhythms and expectations of classroom interaction, and to assume that participation in classroom activities is straightforward. However, for many learners, (neuro)normative social dynamics and expectations can create hidden barriers. While it is important to create opportunities for learners to replicate the kind of (socially normed) interactions they are likely to have outside of the classroom, there is little benefit in setting up practise scenarios that learners cannot access, or that inhibit their learning and self-expression.

Neurodivergent learners, in particular, may differ in how comfortable they feel with group work, small talk, or unstructured discussion, and social interaction itself can be cognitively or emotionally taxing. The following suggested adjustments can help to reduce to social pressure that many neurodivergent learners may experiences, enabling them to particate more fully and develop their interactional language skills more effectively.

Improving access to interaction and participation: Some practical adjustments

- **Provide structure and scaffolding for open-ended interaction tasks:** Small talk and free discussion can be difficult for some neurodivergent learners, especially when expectations are implicit. Providing prompts, examples, roles or guiding questions can make interaction feel more manageable without removing authenticity.
- **Offer alternative interactive formats:** Pair and group work doesn't necessarily have to rely on spontaneous verbal exchange. When open discussion remains difficult for certain learners, consider providing different options for interacting, such as collaborative written tasks or voice note volleys that allow learners to practise interactional language without relying on immediate social performance.
- **Make participation opt-in rather than compulsory where possible:** Allowing learners to choose how and when they contribute can reduce anxiety and support more meaningful engagement over time.
- **Reduce pressure to perform socially:** Not all learners are comfortable sharing their thoughts aloud, improvising, or responding immediately. Building in preparation time or delayed response options can help learners participate while reducing stress and the pressure to mask.

- **Be mindful of social conformity pressures in group work:** Learners may feel pressure to fit in with peers or to mask differences in communication style. Creating explicit permission for different ways of working can help groups function more inclusively.

Improving access to assessment

Many approaches to improving accessibility in assessment align closely with UDL principles, particularly those that emphasise choice and flexibility. When thinking about building flexibility into assessment, a helpful starting point is to reflect on the learning outcomes being assessed, and to consider whether there are alternative ways for learners to demonstrate their learning.

In some cases, a written essay might be easily replaced with an audio or video submission without compromising the assessment aim. If the objective is to demonstrate use of specific vocabulary, grammar or functional language, this flexibility is often appropriate. Where the aim is to assess writing in a particular register or genre, spoken alternatives may not be suitable. However, adjustments can still be made. Suitable adjustments might include allowing the use of dictation software or offering flexibility in how written work is produced (such as typed rather than handwritten). In some contexts, alternative formats, such as recorded presentations or slide-based submissions, may also be appropriate, provided they allow learners to demonstrate the specific skills being assessed. Where writing in a particular register or genre is a core outcome, adjustments should focus on reducing barriers to production rather than changing the nature of the task itself.

In summary

In this final chapter, we have focused on practical ways of making English language learning more accessible by paying attention to how classrooms, materials, tasks and interactions are designed. Just as there are an almost infinite number of English language learners and language learning contexts, there will be an almost infinite number of ways in which you can adapt your teaching for broader accessibility and inclusivity.

Accessibility is not a fixed end point, but an ongoing, reflective practice. Approaching it with flexibility and care can help create classrooms in which more learners are able to participate meaningfully.

TL:DR (too long: didn't read) summary

- UDL highlights how building flexibility and choice into teaching from the outset can improve accessibility for more learners and reduce teacher workload over time.
- At times, learners may still require individual reasonable adjustments or accommodations. These are most effective when they are person-centred, guided by learners, and offered without assuming disclosure or diagnosis. Neurodivergent ELT teachers are part of the profession. The same kinds of adjustments that support learners (such as clarity, flexibility and sensory awareness) can also reduce workplace pressure and burnout for colleagues.
- Access can be improved across many areas of teaching and learning, including the learning environment, tasks and instructions, attention and engagement, social participation and assessment.

Reflective questions

1. Which of the adjustments discussed in this chapter would be easiest to integrate into your current lesson planning and teaching practice? Why?
2. Are there any suggestions that feel difficult to put into practice? If so, what support might you need to implement them, and who could you speak to in order to access that support?

Afterword

Thank you for coming along on this journey with me.

For me, it really does feel like long journey! Finding time to think deeply and to write between work commitments, life's regular surprises and ongoing health issues (which often go hand-in-hand with being neurodivergent) has been harder than I anticipated, and harder than writing my first book. I'm sure there's something in there about the frequent changes of perspective required when you're bridging theory and practice – and how attention-shifting can be harder for neurodivergent people with monotropic attention styles, already overtaxed by the busy lives we all lead. But look, we've both made it to the end of this book! And that is a testament to the powers of interest and perseverance – two of the most important ingredients for improving neurodivergent access to your English language teaching.

Throughout this book, I hope I've conveyed the idea that neurodiversity is an ongoing conversation rather than a finished framework. Public awareness and understanding of neurodivergence have grown rapidly in recent years, and the way we think and talk about neurodiversity continue to evolve. At the time of writing, there was very little published specifically on neurodiversity in ELT – something I'm sure will change quickly, further shaping how we approach neurodiversity-inclusive teaching in the future.

Above all, my aim for this book was to equip you with the knowledge and understanding to work thoughtfully with neurodivergent language learners. No two learners will present with the same needs or strengths, and this book won't have anticipated every kind of neurodivergent experience you may encounter in your teaching career. Hopefully, however, you'll feel able to meet any new challenges head on, grounded in the essential concepts of the neurodiversity paradigm, the social model of disability, and Universal Design for Learning. If ever you feel unsure, ask your learners. They are always the experts in their own experiences.

The fact that you've taken time to read this book is already a fantastic commitment to making your teaching practice more inclusive of neurodivergent learners. Ideas often need time to percolate and there is no need to rush into immediate, drastic changes. As I hope we've seen throughout this book, meaningful change often comes from small, thoughtful adjustments rather than wholesale redesigns of practice. Most importantly, it's not down to individual teachers to make everything work for everyone. Many of the barriers that neurodivergent learners face are systemic, and addressing them requires institutional change and collective effort.

If you've enjoyed this book, or found it useful, consider loaning it to a colleague, or recommend it your head of department or director of studies. *A rising tide lifts all ships, but more hands make light work…*

Appendices

Inclusive learning self-evaluative tool

Adapted from: Wray, M. (2020) *Inclusive Learning, Teaching and Assessment Framework*. York: York St John University. Available online at: https://inclusioninhe.com/projects/iltaf/

In each section below are statements that are indicative of good inclusive practice. Rate yourself against these statements, from 1–5:

- **5 – I do this very well now** and will continue to maintain this level of activity during the next two academic years
- **4 – I have made a good start on this** and will continue to progess activity over the next two academic years
- **3 – I don't know** but will find out and build activity into the action plan this academic year
- **2 – I don't really do this well enough** and need to develop this aspect over the next two academic years
- **1 – I don't address this yet**

Before teaching

- I've explored inclusive pedagogic approaches (e.g. using the 'flipped classroom') as a way to allow students to engage with material and prepare for sessions in advance.
- Students have access to an overview of teaching and learning content and appropriate materials before the teaching session.
- Learning outcomes and assesment methods are made available to all students from the outset of the programme.
- Accessible information about support services is widely available.
- Issues of accessibility during field trips have been pre-empted and resolved.

During teaching

- Barriers to accessing teaching delivery are removed (e.g. subtitles are provided for multi-media or transcripts).
- Learning outcomes are stated at the outset of each session.
- Recording of teaching sessions is permitted (e.g. notetakers, mobile devices, lecture capture).
- Strategies are in place to ensure that **all** students can engage in class activities in equitable ways.
- Students are allowed preparation time when asked to contribute in class discussion.
- Multi-sensory presentation to appeal to multiple learning preferences.

Assessment

- For both formative and summative assessment, a range of approaches are offered for assessing students' learning.
- Courses use appropriate and balanced methods to assess learning outcomes.
- Clear information is provided in advance to students on the assessment methodologies used and the marking schemes employed.
- Students are provided with timely information on assessment (e.g. when and how) and in an accessible format (or range of formats)
- Regular formative assessment opportunities are provided so that students can receive feedback on their progress well in advance of summative assessment. These could include self- and peer-assessment opportunities.

Use the information from this exercise to prioritise your action planning.

UDL audit and planner

Use this planner as a guide to help you audit how UDL principles feature in your current lessons. Try to identify any current challenges to UDL, and think about how you might overcome these.

Reflect on: **materials, assessment tools, the learning environment, your teaching methods**

Choice and flexibility in...	**Strengths** Think about your learners and existing lessons. What already works, and what can you harness further?	**Barriers** What barriers can you anticipate to delivering choice and flexibility in this domain?	**Strategies** What adaptations, adjustments or alternatives could you include to overcome the challenges you've identified and build on student interests?
engagement			
representation			
action and expression			

Implicit bias and neurodiversity: A reflective tool

Unconscious (or 'implicit') biases are social stereotypes about certain groups of people that form outside our conscious awareness. We all carry them – it's part of how human brains make sense of the world.

Stigma and misinformation around neurodivergence are still widespread in media and public discourse, influencing the unconscious biases we may carry. When left unexamined, these hidden assumptions can shape how we think about and treat – or teach – neurodivergent people.

Reflecting on them is the first step to making them visible and changeable. This tool will guide you through that process.

Step 1: Unfiltered first thoughts

Take a moment to notice your initial, unfiltered reactions when you think about teaching neurodivergent pupils. Write down whatever comes to mind: your fears, worries, assumptions or gut feelings. E.g. *Do you assume that a student's learning difference will make your job harder or disrupt the class?*

This is a private reflection that no one else will see (and you can discard it afterwards).

Are you surprised by anything you've written?

Step 2: First impressions

How would you feel about the following learner behaviours? Tick the first answer that comes into your head before you give it much thought.

Answer honestly, this exercise is only for your own private reflection.

	Positively	**Neutrally**	**Negatively**
Minimal eye contact			
Fidgets a lot			
Monotonous prosody			
Perpetual late attender			
Poor or illegible handwriting / messy work			
Takes long conversational turns			
Often seems lost, distracted or disengaged			
Rocks at desk or hums while working			
Rarely contributes			
Completes tasks much more slowly than others			
Consistently poor spelling			

Step 3: Reflecting on neurodivergent biases

Look back over your answers to Step 2. Where you rated a behaviour either negatively or neutrally, take a moment to consider which minority neurotypes these behaviours might be associated with. You may wish to refer back to Chapter 2 to remind yourself of some of key characteristics of different kinds of neurodivergence.

Behaviours rated negatively	→	Associated minority neurotype

Societies are organised around neurotypical norms. We all have implicit biases that are shaped by these norms (as well as many others things).

Noticing what you have recorded above, can you put a name to any potential neurodivergent biases you might have? E.g. a small-talk bias, an active-participation bias, etc. Identifying them this way can help you to notice them better in the moment when they come up, so you can make more informed decisions on how to act.

Step 4: Imagination activity: A day in the life

This final activity is an opportunity to flex your perspective-taking skills.

All of us find it hard to know what it's like to be another person, especially when their lived experiences is very different from our own. However, as English language teachers, we are already quite adept at bridging cultural and communicative differences. By putting ourselves in the shoes of our neurodivergent learners, we can increase our empathy for them and feel better prepared to support their needs.

Firstly, select either one minority neurotype that came up during the earlier steps, or one minority neurotype you feel least familiar with. Imagine a learner with this neurodivergence joins your class. In the spaces below (*or spoken aloud or in your own mind – we're enacting UDL!*), consider how they might experience each of the following scenarios:

Starting their day and finding their way to the new classroom

Experiencing their first day in a new class in a second (*or third...*) language

Being thrown into group work in a busy, brightly lit classroom

Attempting homework at the end of a long, tiring day with minimal instructions or guidance

Bibliography

Act for Eliminating Discrimination against Persons with Disabilities, Japan. (Act No. 65 of June 26, 2013). Available online at: https://www.japaneselawtranslation.go.jp/en/laws/view/4930/

Al-Azawei, A., Serenelli, F. and Lundqvist, K. (2016). Universal Design for Learning (UDL): A content analysis of peer reviewed journals from 2012 to 2015. *Journal of the Scholarship of Teaching and Learning, 16* (3): 39-56

Atkinson, A. (2026) An Interest-Based Exploration of Monotropism and Its Use in the Classroom. In *Neurodivergent Education and Lifelong Learning* (pp.129-146). IGI Global Scientific Publishing.

Bastow, C. and Case, J. (Eds.) (2025) *Someone Like Me: An Anthology of Non-fiction by Autistic Writers.*

Blackwell, A.G. (2017). The Curb-Cut Effect. *Stanford Social Innovation Review.* Available online at: https://ssir.org/articles/entry/the_curb_cut_effect

Bortz, M.A. (20250. Introduction to the Forum: Embracing Neurodiversity: A Global Perspective. *Perspectives of the ASHA Special Interest Groups*, pp.1-6.

Botha, M., Chapman, R., Giwa Onaiwu, M., Kapp, S.K., Stannard Ashley, A. and Walker, N.(2024). The neurodiversity concept was developed collectively: An overdue correction on the origins of neurodiversity theory. *Autism, 28* (6): 1591-1594

Brewer, R., Biotti, F., Catmur, C., Press, C., Happé, F., Cook, R. and Bird, G. (2016) Can neurotypical individuals read autistic facial expressions? Atypical production of emotional facial expressions in autism spectrum disorders. *Autism Research, 9* (2): 262-271

Brissett-Bailey, M. (Ed.) (2023) *Black, Brilliant and Dyslexic: Neurodivergent heroes tell their stories.* Jessica Kingsley Publishers.

British Council (2025) *Teaching for Success: Continuing Professional Development (CPD) Framework for teachers.* Available online at: https://www.teachingenglish.org.uk/sites/teacheng/files/2025-04/CPD%20Framework%20for%20teachers%202025%20-%20Guidance%20Booklet.pdf

Bruno, G. (2023). *The Gift of Being Different* (video). Available online at: https://vimeo.com/817471409

Burgstahler, S. E. (2009). *Universal Design in Education: Principles and Applications.* Seattle, WA: DO-IT, University of Washington Center for Applied Special Technology (CAST) (2024). *UDL Guidelines 3.0.* Available online at: https://udlguidelines.cast.org/more/about-guidelines-3-0/

Chapman, R. *Empire of Normality: Neurodiversity and Capitalism.* Pluto Press.

Crenshaw, Kimberle (1989). Demarginalizing the Intersection of Race and Sex: A Black Feminist Critique of Antidiscrimination Doctrine, Feminist Theory and Antiracist Politics, *University of Chicago Legal Forum: 1* (8): 139-167

Crompton, C.J., Fletcher-Watson, S. and Ropar, D. (2019a) "I never realised everybody felt as happy as I do when I am around autistic people": a thematic analysis of autistic adults' relationships with autistic and neurotypical friends and family. *Autism, 24* (6): 1443

Csecs, J.L., Iodice, V., Rae, C.L., Brooke, A., Simmons, R., Quadt, L., Savage, G.K., Dowell, N.G., Prowse, F., Themelis, K. and Mathias, C.J. (2022). Joint hypermobility links neurodivergence to dysautonomia and pain. *Frontiers in Psychiatry, 12*, p.786916

Davidson, J. and Tamas, S. (2016). Autism and the ghost of gender. *Emotion, Space and Society, 19*: 59-65

Equality Act (2010) UK. Available online at: https://www.legislation.gov.uk/ukpga/2010/15/contents

European Commission. (2025). *European Accessibility Act.* Available online at: https://commission.europa.eu/strategy-and-policy/policies/justice-and-fundamental-rights/disability/union-equality-strategy-rights-persons-disabilities-2021-2030/european-accessibility-act_en

Federal Law No. 29 of 2006 Concerning the Rights of Persons with Special Needs, United Arab Emirates. Available online at: https://www.mohesr.gov.ae/En/Legislation/Pages/default.aspx

George, R. and Stokes, M.A. (2018). Gender identity and sexual orientation in autism spectrum disorder. *Autism, 22* (8): 970-982

Gernsbacher, M.A., Morson, E.M. and Grace, E.J. (2016) Language and speech in autism. *Annual Review of Linguistics*, 2: 413-425

Goulardins, J.B., Rigoli, D., Licari, M., Piek, J.P., Hasue, R.H., Oosterlaan, J. and Oliveira, J.A. (2015). Attention deficit hyperactivity disorder and developmental coordination disorder: Two separate disorders or do they share a common etiology. *Behavioural Brain Research, 292*: 484-492

Gowen, E. and Hamilton, A. (2013). Motor abilities in autism: a review using a computational context. *Journal of autism and developmental disorders, 43* (2): 323-344

Grant et al. (2025): "A lovely safe umbrella to describe yourself with" or "meaningless": an online survey of UK-based Neurodivergent adults' views of neurodiversity-related terminology. *Neurodiversity 3*, p.27546330251390590

Grant, S., Norton, S., Weiland, R.F., Scheeren, A.M., Begeer, S. and Hoekstra, R.A. (2022). Autism and chronic ill health: an observational study of symptoms and diagnoses of central sensitivity syndromes in autistic adults. *Molecular Autism, 13* (1), p.7

Griffiths, S., Allison, C., Kenny, R., Holt, R., Smith, P., & Baron Cohen, S. (2019). The Vulnerability Experiences Quotient (VEQ): A study of vulnerability, mental health and life satisfaction in autistic adults. *Autism Research, 12* (10): 1516–1528

Harris, M.E. and Fallot, R.D. (2001) *Using trauma theory to design service systems*. Jossey-Bass/Wiley.

Heasman, B. and Gillespie, A. (2018) Perspective-taking is two-sided: Misunderstandings between people with Asperger's syndrome and their family members. *Autism, 22* (6): 740-750

Heasman, B. and Gillespie, A., (2019) Neurodivergent intersubjectivity: Distinctive features of how autistic people create shared understanding. *Autism, 23* (4): 910-921

Hillary, A., 2020. Autist/biography. In *The Palgrave handbook of auto/biography* (pp. 315-339). Cham: Springer International Publishing

Hours, C., Recasens, C. and Baleyte, J.M. (2022). ASD and ADHD comorbidity: What are we talking about?. *Frontiers in Psychiatry, 13*, p.837424

Hutchins, T.L., Knox, S.E. and Fletcher, E.C., 2024. Natural language acquisition and gestalt language processing: A critical analysis of their application to autism and speech language therapy. *Autism & Developmental Language Impairments, 9*, p.23969415241249944

Hutson, T.M., Hassrick, E.M., Fernandes, S., Walton, J., Bouvier-Weinberg, K., Radcliffe, A. and Allen-Handy, A. (2022). "I'm just different–that's all–I'm so sorry…": Black men, ASD and the urgent need for DisCrit Theory in police encounters. *Policing: An International Journal, 45* (3): 524-537

Jallow, L. (2025). Neurodivergence Was Supported, Not Pathologized, *The Lovette Jallow Perspective (on Substack)*. Published, Apr 25, 2025. Available online at: https://lovettejallow.substack.com/p/neurodivergence-ancient-africa

Jenkins, J., Cogo, A. and Dewey, M. (2011) Review of developments in research into English as a lingua franca. *Language Teaching, 44* (3): 281-315

Kampoureli, C.N., Rae, C.L., Van Praag, C.G., Harrison, N.A., Garfinkel, S.N., Critchley, H.D. and Eccles, J.A., 2025. Neural processes linking joint hypermobility and anxiety: key roles for the amygdala and insular cortex. *The British Journal of Psychiatry*, pp.1-7

Kanner, L. (1943) Autistic disturbances of affective contact. *Nervous Child, 2* (3): 217- 250

Kapp, S.K. (ed.) (2020) *Autistic community and the neurodiversity movement: Stories from the frontline* (p. 330). Springer Nature / Palgrave MacMillan.

Lai, M.C., Amestoy, A., Bishop, S., Brown, H.M., Onaiwu, M.G., Halladay, A., Harrop, C., Hotez, E., Huerta, M., Kelly, A. and Miller, D (2023). Improving autism identification and support for individuals assigned female at birth: clinical suggestions and research priorities. *The Lancet Child & Adolescent Health, 7* (12): 897-908

Lewis, M., 1993. *The Lexical Approach* (Vol. 1, p. 993). Hove: Language Teaching Publications.

Loomes, R., Hull, L. and Mandy, W.P.L. (2017). What is the male-to-female ratio in autism spectrum disorder? A systematic review and meta-analysis. *Journal of the American Academy of Child & Adolescent Psychiatry, 56* (6): 466-474

Martin, N., Wray, M. and Krupa, J. (2025). *Universal Design for Learning: A Critical Approach.* London and New York: Routledge

Martino, D., Ganos, C. and Pringsheim, T.M. (2017). Tourette syndrome and chronic tic disorders: the clinical spectrum beyond tics. *International Review of Neurobiology, 134*: 1461-1490

McDonough, K., Liu, C. and Trofimovich, P. (2023) Strategies for avoiding misunderstanding in English L2 conversations. *ELT Journal, 77* (4): 426-434

Merscher, J., Barra, S., Xander, A.M., Patrasc, P.G., Retz-Junginger, P. and Retz, W. (2025). Adult ADHD predicts intimate partner violence perpetration and victimization irrespective of gender and age. *Scientific Reports, 15* (1), p.4914

Milton, D.E. (2012). On the ontological status of autism: The 'double empathy problem'. *Disability & society, 27* (6): 883-887

Milton, D.E. (2017). *A Mismatch of Salience.* Hove: Pavilion Publishing

Motteram, G. & Dawson, S. (2025). What's changed in English Language Teaching? A review of change in the teaching and learning of English and in teacher education and development from 2014-2024 *British Council.* https://doi.org/10.57884/FPE8-5130

Nair, V.K., Farah, W. and Boveda, M. (2024). Is neurodiversity a global northern white paradigm?. *Autism*, p.13623613241280835

Nelson, T. (2024). *"Before people see the autism, they see my race": An intersectional exploration of the lived experiences of masking and camouflaging Black Autistic girls in UK education using IPA and DisCrit* (Doctoral dissertation, University of Essex & Tavistock and Portman NHS Foundation Trust).

Newman, I. and Conway, J. (2017) Busting the barriers to inclusive learning environments. *The Journal of Inclusive Practice in Further and Higher Education*, p.33.

Office for Health Improvement and Disparities (OHID) (2022) *Working definition of trauma-informed practice.* (Published 2 November 2022). Available at: https://www.gov.uk/government/publications/working-definition-of-trauma-informed-practice

Office for National Statistics (ONS). (2019). *Disability and crime, UK: 2019.* [online] Available at: https://www.ons.gov.uk/peoplepopulationandcommunity/healthandsocialcare/disability/bulletins/disabilityandcrimeuk/2019

Oliver, M. (1983) Social Work with Disabled People. *Practical Social Work Series*, BASW.

Pearson, A. and Rose, K. (2023). *Autistic Masking: Understanding Identity Management and the Role of Stigma.* Pavilion Publishing

Pearson, A., Grant, A., Leigh, J., Macdonald, S., Williams, K., Williams, G., Spaeth, E., Rose, K., Memmott, A. and Botha, M. (2025: pre-print). "It's like calling short people vertically challenged": Language and terminology preferences among neurodivergent adults.

Rose, K. (2024). What is Neurodiversity? (blog article). *The Autistic Advocate.* Published September 3, 2024. Available online at: https://theautisticadvocate.com/what-is-neurodiversity-new/

Rumball, F., Brook, L., Happé, F. and Karl, A. (2021). Heightened risk of posttraumatic stress disorder in adults with autism spectrum disorder: The role of cumulative trauma and memory deficits. *Research in Developmental Disabilities, 110*, p.103848

Sasson, N.J., Faso, D.J., Nugent, J., Lovell, S., Kennedy, D.P. and Grossman, R.B. (2017) Neurotypical peers are less willing to interact with those with autism based on thin slice judgments. *Scientific Reports, 7* (1): 40700

Schmidt, R. (1990). The Role of Consciousness in Second Language Learning. *Applied Linguistics*, 11: 129-158

Sheppard, E., Pillai, D., Wong, G.T.L., Ropar, D. and Mitchell, P. (2016) How easy is it to read the minds of people with autism spectrum disorder? *Journal of Autism and Developmental Disorders, 46* (4): 1247-1254

Singer, J. (1999). 'Why can't you be normal for once in your life? From a 'problem with no name' to a new category of disability'. In M. Corker & S. French (Eds.), *Disability Discourse* (pp. 59–67). Open University Press

Spencer, A. E., Faraone, S. V., Bogucki, O. E., Pope, A. L., Uchida, M., Milad, M. R., Spencer, T. J., Woodworth, K. Y., & Biederman, J. (2016). Examining the association between posttraumatic stress disorder and attention-deficit/hyperactivity disorder: a systematic review and meta-analysis. *The Journal of Clinical Psychiatry, 77* (1), 72–83

Sterponi, L. and de Kirby, K. (2016) A multidimensional reappraisal of language in autism: Insights from a discourse analytic study. *Journal of Autism and Developmental Disorders*, 46 (2): 394-405

Story, M. F., Mueller, J. L., & Mace, R. L. (1998). *The Universal Design File: Designing for People of All Ages and Abilities.* Raleigh, NC: Center for Universal Design, North Carolina State University

Swain, M. (2006). Languaging, agency and collaboration in advanced second language learning. In H. Byrnes (Ed.), *Advanced language learning: The contributions of Halliday and Vygotsky* (p.98). London, England: Continuum

TESOL DEIA Initiative (2021). Available online at: https://www.tesol.org/about/deia-initiative/

The Centre for Excellence in Universal Design (2025) *The 7 Principles* (webpage). Available at: https://universaldesign.ie/about-universal-design/the-7-principles

UNICEF (2017). *Inclusive Education: Understanding Article 24 of the Convention on the Rights of Persons with Disabilities.* Available online at: https://www.unicef.org/eca/sites/unicef.org.eca/files/IE_summary_accessible_220917_0.pdf

United Nations (2006). *Convention on the Rights of Persons with Disabilities.* New York, 13 December 2006, Treaty Series, vol. 2515, p. 3. Available at: https://social.desa.un.org/issues/disability/crpd/convention-on-the-rights-of-persons-with-disabilities-crpd

United States Congress. (1990). *Americans with Disabilities Act of 1990*, Pub. L. No. 101-336, 104 Stat. 327. (Amended by the ADA Amendments Act of 2008, Pub. L. No. 110-325, 122 Stat. 3553). Available online at: https://www.ada.gov/

United States Congress. (2004). *Individuals with Disabilities Education Improvement Act of 2004*, Pub. L. No. 108-446, 118 Stat. 2647. (Originally enacted as the Education for All Handicapped Children Act, 1975, Pub. L. No. 94-142.) Available online at: https://sites.ed.gov/idea/

Walker, N. (2021) *Neuroqueer heresies: Notes on the neurodiversity paradigm, autistic empowerment, and postnormal possibilities.* Fort Worth, TX: Autonomous Press.

Weir, E., Allison, C. and Baron-Cohen, S. (2021). The sexual health, orientation, and activity of autistic adolescents and adults. *Autism Research, 14* (11): 2342-2354

Williams, G. (2024). *Understanding Others in a Neurodiverse World: A Radical Perspective on Communication and Shared Meaning*. Hove: Pavilion Publishing

Wray, M. (2020). *Inclusive Learning, Teaching and Assessment Framework*. York: York St John University. Available online at: https://inclusioninhe.com/projects/iltaf/

Young, S., Adamo, N., Ásgeirsdóttir, B.B., Branney, P., Beckett, M., Colley, W., Cubbin, S., Deeley, Q., Farrag, E., Gudjonsson, G. and Hill, P. (2020). Females with ADHD: An expert consensus statement taking a lifespan approach providing guidance for the identification and treatment of attention-deficit/hyperactivity disorder in girls and women. *BMC Psychiatry*, *20* (1), p.404

Yu, L., Stronach, S. and Harrison, A.J. (2020). Public knowledge and stigma of autism spectrum disorder: Comparing China with the United States. *Autism*, *24* (6): 1531-1545

Please let us know what you thought about

English Language Teaching in a Neurodiverse World

and leave a review

on our website

or amazon.co.uk